THE LIFE
OF DAD

THE LIFE OF DAD

THE MAKING OF THE MODERN FATHER

DR ANNA MACHIN

**SIMON &
SCHUSTER**

London · New York · Sydney · Toronto · New Delhi

A CBS COMPANY

First published in Great Britain by Simon & Schuster UK Ltd, 2018
A CBS COMPANY

3 5 7 9 10 8 6 4 2

Simon & Schuster UK Ltd
1st Floor
222 Gray's Inn Road
London WC1X 8HB

www.simonandschuster.co.uk
www.simonandschuster.com.au
www.simonandschuster.co.in

Simon & Schuster Australia, Sydney
Simon & Schuster India, New Delhi

A CIP catalogue record for this book
is available from the British Library

Paperback ISBN: 978-1-4711-6140-7
eBook ISBN: 978-1-4711-6142-1

Typeset in the UK by M Rules
Printed and bound by CPI Group (UK) Ltd, Croydon, CR0 4YY

For Julian

CONTENTS

Preface

I am often asked why a woman would want to research and write about fathers. Well, the short answer is that I am married to one. Ten years ago, I gave birth to my first child and three years later my second. It turns out that giving birth is not one of my strong points, and the first birth in particular was a long-drawn-out drama resulting in a very sick mother and a very sick baby. Following this birth experience, I was offered counselling and support to deal with my expected trauma, but my husband – who had witnessed everything while I floated around, oblivious in a sea of morphine – was roundly ignored.

Now, I have to make it clear here, or I will be in trouble, that my husband did not expect any support, believing that the focus should rightly be placed on me and our baby. But a year on, when I returned to work and my husband still could not speak of our daughter's birth without showing significant emotional distress, I began to get angry. Angry that my husband, the co-parent of my child, had witnessed a trauma akin to watching a loved one involved in a horrific car crash, but that at no point did anyone ask him if he was okay, if he needed some help. So, being an academic, I did what academics do best and turned to the research literature to find out what my fellow scientists knew about fathers and their experiences.

The answer was: very little. Yes, there was extensive literature assessing the impact of the feckless, absent father on his children, but with respect to the experience of the dedicated, involved dad who changes the nappies, coaches football practice, masters the French plait and chases away the bedtime monsters, the literature was silent. There is no doubt that there are a tiny minority of fathers, as there are mothers, who are defined by their absence – and their negative influence on their children's development is real and critical. But there is a much, much larger contingent of fathers who stick around and do their best, and they also deserve to be recognized and understood. So, I made this my mission. To research the experience of fathers who were present in their children's lives. To write their story from the positive rather than the negative angle.

Since my first rather eventful introduction to parenthood a decade ago, I have dedicated my professional life to researching first-hand the experiences of new fathers. The dads I have studied have come from all walks of life and backgrounds; gay and straight, professional and manual workers, school-leavers and university-educated, and a diversity of ethnic backgrounds. They have allowed me into their lives at one of the most personal and private moments; the moment they became fathers for the first time. I have visited them in the weeks prior to the birth, when they are excited and maybe anxious, but when the future is largely unknown, and returned in the first precious weeks, when excitement is replaced by overwhelmed awe at the tiny thing that has entered their life and turned it upside down. I have analysed their hormones, watched their behaviours, assessed their mental and physical health and studied their brains, often over many months. I have interviewed them over numerous cups of coffee, often with baby joining in as well. The voices you will read throughout this book are theirs, relating their thoughts, feelings and experiences. I hope that hearing these real men talk will help those of you who may be following in their footsteps to feel reassured about your own emotions or experiences, and that they will make the scientific studies I recount more relevant to all our lives.

By allowing me into their lives and that of their families I, and my colleagues, have discovered many unexpected and wonderful things about today's dad. That his role is unique and separate to that of mum, and that this difference is vital to the healthy development of his child. That lots of modern Western fathers want to be fully paid-up members of the co-parenting club, but struggle with a lack of support and information and a society that is not yet ready to accept them in this role. That the role of a father is a complex mix of history, culture and politics, but that a man's biology plays a much bigger part than was originally thought in influencing what sort of father he will be. And that fathers are wonderfully flexible creatures, capable of altering their role on a minute-by-minute basis to ensure the well-being and survival of their family.

So, I have written this book for three reasons. Firstly, to rebalance the record on fathers. To counteract the remorselessly negative press about absent fathers with a positive message about the power and value of the stick-around dad. Secondly, to help those men who might be right at the start of their fatherhood journey. I hope the information I provide and the voices of the real fathers that pepper this book help you feel more secure and comfortable with what lies ahead. And thirdly, and maybe most importantly, I think all dads, and the wider world, have a right to know – and should know – about what is happening to them biologically, psychologically and emotionally. According to the UK Office for National Statistics, there were just over 6 million involved dads in the UK in 2015, the last year for which we have figures. Isn't it about time we knew something about them?

In the first chapter, we will return to the world of 500,000 years ago to meet the very first human father and explore why his revolutionary appearance still has much to tell us about the role and importance of today's modern dad. In Chapter Two, we will explore the powerful bond that forms between father and child even *before* he or she is born and the pre-birth hormones that begin to shape both parents during pregnancy. We will consider what being a father means to the expectant dad and how this new role can allow a man to make much-needed changes in his life and take on a welcome new identity. In Chapter Three, we will visit other countries to see how dads do it there and begin to understand how diverse and wonderful the role of a dad can be. We will explore the pre-eminence of the social rather than biological father in some societies and chart the changing face of the human family, as the liberalization of adoption laws and developments in assisted fertility techniques has meant that even in the West the nuclear family is no longer necessarily the norm. At times, this whirlwind global tour may seem a long way from our experience, but it will enable us to understand that being a dad is about presence and action rather than just genetics.

In Chapter Four, we will focus on dads' experiences of birth and the health of new fathers, including the worrying increase in poor mental health that requires our urgent attention for the good of the man, his family and society. In Chapter Five, we will look at the two pillars of unique responsibility – protection and teaching – which have been at the centre of fathering for half a million years and are still relevant today. We will see that there are as many ways to father as there are fathers, and that a dad's role is defined by his flexibility, but that at their core all dads are focused on responding successfully to the risks that may negatively affect their child's chance of survival. In Chapter Six, with the influence of culture, history, politics and ecology fully acknowledged, we will focus on what a man's individual biology and psychology bring to the fathering table; how his genes, hormone levels and childhood shape the sort of father he will be. We will look at how a dad's genes can influence his sensitivity, how his personality can make even the most difficult child a dream to raise and how his own parents' behaviour can be reflected in his parenting choices. In Chapter Seven, we will explore the fundamental, lifelong attachment between father and child and consider how the need for interaction to build this relationship in the first instance leads to the most wonderful role for boisterous play. But we will also learn how, in the absence of the neuro-chemical experience of childbirth and because of the slow rate of baby's development, this bond can be slow to form. The message here is not to panic – the bond will come.

In Chapter Eight, we will broaden our focus and include a dad's partner. By looking at the brains of mum and dad, we will understand how evolution has shaped them to make sure both parents fulfil their child's developmental needs without needless overlap. We will consider what impact adding a baby (or two, or three . . .) has on the parents' relationship and explore how you both can invest time to make sure your relationship emerges unscathed – hopefully even enhanced – at the other end. In Chapters Nine and Ten, we will look at what a father brings to his child's development; his unique role in teaching, encouraging independence and social autonomy and working to prevent his child suffering from poor mental health in the future. Finally, in Chapter Eleven, we will conclude with a consideration of where we are. After half a million years of evolution, who does today's dad want to be and is society doing all it can to support him in achieving his goal? How can 'Team Dad' – the academics, campaigners and politicized dads who promote involved fathering – encourage the fundamental changes in our culture that are required before all those dads who wish to will truly be able to call themselves co-parents?

This book isn't a 'how to' manual. It won't tell you how to change a nappy or construct a cot, or reveal the elusive cure for colic. But what I hope it will do is give the most up-to-date answer to the question of what being a father is like and give a few tips and hints along the way that make the transition to fatherhood as easy and enjoyable as possible for those who are about to undertake it. For the rest of us, who may be some way down the family road, I hope it is an entertaining read about a person who – regardless of our relationship with them – we all have, or have had, in our lives, however long their presence may have lasted. For established fathers, I hope it mirrors some of your experiences, normalizes some of your worries and explains some of your instincts and behaviours. For mums, I hope it gives you a fascinating and helpful insight into who your partner is. And for the more scientifically minded, I hope the most up-to-date research in the fields of neuroscience, genetics, psychology, endocrinology and health keeps you fully satiated. Much of the research I will tell you about, because of the relative youth of the field, has been focused on the heterosexual nuclear family, but in many cases their findings apply to all fathers. And as the diversity of fathers becomes clearer, we are starting to widen our field of view to include gay dads and families with multiple fathers. Be assured that where these studies exist, I will tell you about them.

By the end of the book, I hope to show you what a complex but significant role being a father is and how a man is fundamentally changed by his fathering experience. But first, to understand the role of the modern dad, we must return to the beginning, the world of half a million years ago and the very first father.

A Note on the Dads

Throughout this book you will hear the voices of real fathers. Over the past ten years, all of them have afforded me the great privilege of studying them as they become dads. Because my work focuses on the early years of a child's life – the period when a father arguably undergoes the most change and asserts the greatest influence on his child's development – the fathers you will meet are speaking during the first five years of their child's life. The nature of my studies means that I have known some fathers for only brief periods of time, while others have let me follow them and their families for the entire five years. Because of this, some took part in interviews more than once. Where this has happened, I have told you how old their child or children were at the time of that particular interview, so you can understand their thought processes at that specific stage of their fathering journey. All of the dads' names, and the names of their children and partners, have been changed to protect their anonymity. I am indebted to the dads who volunteer for my studies and offer them my eternal thanks.

PART ONE

The First Father

CHAPTER ONE

Dad 1.0

The Evolution of Human Fatherhood

It is a little-known fact, but fathers saved the human race.

Five hundred thousand years ago, one of our ancestors, *Homo heidelbergensis*, faced a dilemma. A million years previously, they had left Africa and spread across Europe and the Near East. They had even managed to reach the south coast of England and make their home beside a beautiful, tropical lagoon near what is now the West Sussex village of Boxgrove. Like other hominins of the time, they walked on two legs, but what set them apart from their peers was their ever-expanding brains. They were beginning to form the rudiments of language and had started to innovate, creating beautiful, symmetrical stone tools and perfectly balanced wooden hunting spears. But they faced a problem. They undoubtedly had the potential to succeed as a species, but the two-legged gait and associated narrow pelvises that had given them the endurance to leave Africa, combined with the large heads housing the complex

3

brains that had allowed them to populate new environments, had left them inching towards a demographic time bomb. In order to allow their large heads to fit through their mothers' narrowed birth canals, the babies of *Homo heidelbergensis* were born early, in a highly dependent and vulnerable state.

The question arose, who could mothers turn to to help them with their energetic toddlers while they focused their efforts on the energy-sapping needs of their helpless newborns? How could they raise their children to independence but still reproduce often enough to replace and expand the species? For the first million years or so, grandmas, aunties and sisters filled the gap. But then, 500,000 years ago, with our friend *Homo heidelbergensis*, the hominin brain took another large leap in size and suddenly girl power was not enough. So, who stepped in? Dad. He harnessed his new skill of controlling fire to cook hard-to-digest plants, thereby enabling his toddlers to eat solid food and allowing his partner to focus on their newborn, and he hunted for the high-value game that fuelled his energy-hungry family. He adopted the role of teacher so that his teenage children learnt the essential survival skills of tool production, predator defence and hunting, and obtained the complex social skills that enabled them to cooperate with their fellow hunters. The result: our ancestors were saved from possible extinction, and half a million years later we are one of the most successful animals on the planet, yet we are members of the exclusive club of 5 per cent of mammal species – and the only ape – whose males invest in their offspring. Human fatherhood was born.

* * *

Evolutionary anthropologists are obsessed with what makes us human. What separates us from the other animals and, in particular, our fellow great apes? Defining the difference anatomically isn't that tricky – you don't need me to tell you that it is unlikely you would confuse your two-legged, largely hairless fellow man for a gorilla, except possibly on the darkest of nights, after a good evening in the pub. But, if we consider the difference behaviourally, defining where chimp becomes man becomes considerably more difficult. We once thought that it was the ability to make tools – after all, the stone tools that litter the 2-million-year-old archaeological sites of East Africa undoubtedly herald a striking change in behaviour and intelligence; but wild chimps have shown themselves to be well versed in using stone tools to crack nuts and fallen leaves to sponge up much-needed water. Even our language skills, once thought to be the marker of our unique intelligence, have been shown to exist in lab-trained chimps, who can use a range of signs to express their needs and emotions and even produce simple sentences. It is fair to say these sentences are often largely restricted to food-related requests, but they can communicate none the less. What is often overlooked is the one behaviour without which our species would simply no longer exist: fatherhood.

Among mammals, fathers who stick around and help care for their offspring are a rare beast. Among birds, the father who diligently flies miles a day back and forth to the nest to provide his youngsters with food is common – in over 90 per cent of bird species, both mum and dad invest time and energy in their brood. But in mammals, the more common behaviour is male promiscuity – males mate with a number of females and often don't stick around much beyond the act of copulation itself. Our closest ape cousins practise promiscuity in two distinct ways. Gorillas exhibit a one male/many female strategy: the harem system. This means that the large silverback male keeps all the females to himself unless a younger, less dominant male manages to sneak a quick mating in behind a tree when he's not looking. The gorilla father does look benignly on his many offspring, as he is virtually assured of their paternity, but his input into their actual care is zero. The existence of a food-rich environment, the relatively fast development of gorilla babies and long periods between births means that mothers are able to provide all the care a gorilla baby needs – dad can add little to the mix. In chimpanzees, the living arrangements are more liberal, with multiple males mating with multiple females in a large group – although the alpha male will still get access to the most and best females. None of the males know which of the many youngsters are theirs and, as a consequence, they do not expend any precious energy on them. Rather, time is better spent grooming fellow males, building up all-important alliances and taking part in the complex chimp politics that ensure a male's place in the chimp hierarchy.

In contrast, human apes have evolved a very different model of fathering, where dads stick around to help out with their children. How they achieve this varies widely between cultures, something that we will explore later in this book, but at the end of the day they all play a critical role in their children's lives. And the need for their involvement began with the unique combination of the two anatomical features – bipedalism and big brains – I mentioned earlier. For, if you are a quadruped – that is, you walk on four legs – your legs are arranged rather like the legs of a table, each at a considerable distance from the other, at the corners of your body. In contrast, the legs of a biped are close together, meaning that we have a much deeper and narrower pelvis and, as a result, birth canal than our four-legged friends. In itself, this narrowing of the birth canal is not an issue, but combine it with a large brain and you quickly hit a problem.

In terms of development, animal babies can emerge from the womb behaving in one of two ways: either very advanced, with eyes and ears open, fur or hair developed and ready to move around independently soon after birth; or helpless, unable to move, with eyes and ears closed. The first category of development is called precocial – from which we get the word 'precocious' – and it is the usual state of affairs for ape babies. It still astounds me how adeptly a chimp baby can climb unaided through the trees only a few days after birth. The second category is labelled altricial, and you will recognize it as the experience of puppies and kittens. These two paths of growth exist because, in the vast majority of species, the growth of the baby's brain happens at one of two times: either in the womb – the chimp model – or after birth, as happens in puppies and kittens. I say the vast majority of species because there is one exception. Us.

Human brains are significantly larger than would be expected for a mammal of our body weight – nearly six times larger, in fact. And it is this anatomical attribute that has enabled us to be so successful. We have developed language, exhibited an unsurpassed ability to innovate and are capable of commanding a level of control over our environment that has enabled us to dominate the earth. But because we have such unusually large brains for our body size, we need longer for our brains to grow. And herein lies the problem. Our narrowed pelvis means that this crucial period of development cannot occur in the womb because it would be impossible for the baby to travel successfully through our narrowed birth canal – indeed, both the mother and baby would be at significant risk of death. So, to ensure the survival of the species, evolution has selected for humans to have an unusually short gestation length, meaning that human babies are born before they are fully developed. This results in two outcomes: one, that human babies display a combination of characteristics at birth – the helplessness of a puppy but the open eyes and ears of a chimp; and two, that humans are the only species that exhibits a period of significant brain growth both before *and* after birth. Problem solved.

But is it? Allowing a period of significant brain growth after birth, one year in our case, allows the brain to reach its full potential, but it does mean that the mother has a considerable burden to deal with; a very dependent, immobile, energy-hungry baby. Not only must she expend considerable energy carrying her offspring but, theoretically, she should also have to breastfeed it for longer than would be the case if her baby's period of brain growth occurred only *before* birth, as occurs in chimps. But, in reality, this is not the case. While in some societies human mothers will breastfeed beyond six months, it is wholly possible, and the norm within the West, to wean a baby onto solid food when it reaches this age. Why do humans display such a short period of lactation?

It is all down to demographics and the survival of the

species. The evolution of the shortened periods of gestation and lactation probably evolved around the same time, 1.8 million years ago with the evolution of *Homo ergaster*. Solely breastfeeding prevents a mother becoming pregnant again, evolution's way of making sure all her time and energy is committed to the needs of her growing baby. But if our ancestors had been committed to doing this to the extent required by the post-birth development of the human brain – the most energy-hungry organ in our body, even when it's not growing – it would have meant that the time between human births was so long that the species was unable to replace itself. Our ancestors would have become extinct and maybe another species would have come to dominate the earth. But by reducing the amount of time that they breastfeed, mothers could stop feeding their children earlier, become fertile again and ensure that they were producing babies at a rate sufficient to maintain, and indeed enlarge, the population.

Any parent can relate to the overwhelmed feeling engendered by trying to juggle the needs of a newborn baby with the incessant demands of a toddler to be fed, cuddled, comforted and played with. I remember the stress involved in trying to breastfeed my second child while struggling to locate the right *Teletubbies* DVD and produce a drink and snack for my firstborn. You become very adept at doing everything one-handed. But imagine this with all the advantages that modern life has bestowed upon us removed – no labour-saving devices, baby equipment and family-planning methods. This was the lot of the prehistoric female *Homo ergaster*. Without the capacity to control her own reproduction from the age of sexual maturity, around eleven to thirteen years of age, she would be constantly either pregnant or breastfeeding a newborn and trying to deal with any number of dependent toddlers. Not for her the leisurely five-year period between births common in the chimpanzee.

* * *

Humans are defined by the extraordinary extent of our cooperation. Think how many times a day you interact with a fellow human to achieve a goal. We cooperate to find or produce the food and water resources that are vital for our survival, to teach and learn the skills and knowledge to live and be successful, to trade, and to raise our children. One of the most powerful forms of cooperation is that between genetic relatives, or kin. This is known as kin selection, and it relies on the fact that by helping those to whom we are blood-related we are benefiting our own survival. In the main, this is not because by helping our kin we can expect help in return when we need it, although this is often the case, but because we share genes and, as any good evolutionary biologist knows, the survival of these genes is ultimately all that matters. This is the concept of the 'selfish gene', first labelled and explored by Richard Dawkins in his 1976 book of the same name, and it proposes that the unit of inheritance on which evolution acts is not the individual but the gene. So, by helping a relative care for their children we ensure the survival of those children and, by association, versions of our own genes. It goes without saying that the closer the relative is to you in blood terms, the more advantageous it is for you to help them with their children, as the number of genes you share with them is greater. Hence it is nearly universally the case that grandparents are the most likely to care for grandchildren after the children's own parents.

So, it is to her kin that our female *Homo ergaster* would have turned in her hour of need. Whether it was, in fact, her mother is debatable, as it is unclear if the lifespan of our ancestors was sufficient to allow anyone to reach the ripe old age of grandparenthood. Despite millennia of evolution, the age of menopause has always been around fifty years of age and the frequency of skeletons of this age in the fossil record is notably low, if not non-existent (arguing over this point fills many happy hours for anthropologists – we are a strange breed). But we know that it would have been some form of *female* kin. How do we know this? Because evolution is *parsimonious*, that is, it will always achieve its end point by the least complicated and/or least expensive route. In all cases, it is energetically less costly to cooperate with someone of the same sex than someone of the opposite sex. I think we can all relate to this. This is because by cooperating with someone of the same sex, you are using the same currency of exchange, making acts of cooperation easy to follow. Even among kin, cooperation is expected to be more or less reciprocal – you scratch my back and I will scratch yours – so keeping track of the acts of cooperation is essential to make sure that you are not always the one offering help. And the easier it is to do this, the less brain power is involved and the less precious energy is consumed. In the evolutionary past, when it came to children, women exchanged the same types of act, namely those associated with the care or

11

protection of the child. For men, the reasons were different – they might help with a child because they hoped it would increase their chances of being mum's next partner, a very different form of currency. This made the exchange rate between the two forms of currency incredibly complicated to calculate, so evolution decreed that we avoided having to make these exchanges unless we *absolutely* had to. As a consequence, mothers sought out other women to help them in the first instance.

So, there our female *Homo ergaster* was, raising her children with the help of her female relatives; her sisters, cousins and even elder daughters. As we know, for over a million years such help sufficed, but around 500,000 years ago, with the second large increase in brain size, the energetic costs of raising an infant again became too much to cope with. This huge leap in brain size, to close to the 1,300 cubic centimetres of today, meant that the period of child dependency became even longer and the requirement for very high-energy food – in this case, meat – became even more pressing. Up until now, meat had been obtained in a rather haphazard manner; by scavenging the kills of carnivores or by the (very exciting-sounding) practice of power-scavenging – stealing a fresh kill from the still very present predator. But it was clear that this ad hoc method was no longer sufficient, and more predict-able and considerably less dangerous methods of obtaining this vital resource would need to be developed to feed this enormous brain. It is no coincidence that with the emergence of the bigger-brained *Homo heidelbergensis* we also see the first consistent evidence in the archaeological record for hunting spears. And not any old hunting spears, but 5-foot-long, perfectly crafted wooden javelins such as those recovered from the 450,000-year-old site of Schöningen in Germany. *Homo heidelbergensis* was not only a skilled hunter but also a highly skilled craftsman.

It was no longer the case that female relatives, all of whom were likely to be nursing their own dependent children, could band together to raise their children alone. The need for reliable sources of meat to feed fast-developing toddlers and provide the mother with adequate nutrition to meet the increasing energetic demands of gestating and breastfeeding her large-brained infants meant that someone else needed to step in to ensure the survival of the species. Someone with the time, energy and skill to hunt for meat and produce efficient hunting and butchery tools. Someone not hindered by the energy-sapping processes of reproduction but still bound by the bonds of genetic relatedness. Someone who could build hearths – an explosion of which occurs in the archaeological record at this time – and control fire, enabling the meat gained by hunting to be cooked, making it easier for small stomachs to digest. Someone who could make it their role, as the children grew and became adolescents, to pass on the skills of tool production and the rules of the hunt. And as hunts became more complex, someone who could teach the vital communication and cooperation skills that were so critical both to the success of the hunt and to the child's success in the wider social world. And as we know from the introduction to this chapter, that person was dad.

* * *

Unlike our ape cousins, the difference in size between the modern human sexes is relatively small. Men are about 1.1 times bigger than women, while male gorillas are nearly twice as big as females, at 1.75 times as large. This large size is a consequence of the male gorilla's need to defend his harem of breeding females from other males. In contrast, for the last half a million years we have lived largely as monogamous pairs, where both sexes exercise choice as to who they want to be with; there is no need for men to use physical strength to corral multiple females who have little choice as to who their male partner may be. This closeness in size is critical in the evolution of human fatherhood. In a very neat analysis, evolutionary anthropologist Dr Cathy Key of University College London used this difference in size between the sexes to calculate when human fatherhood emerged. In most species where males are considerably larger than females, the costs of reproduction to a male are significantly higher than those to a female, as he needs to grow and maintain a large body to ensure successful access to mates. However, in humans the costs to a man of reproducing are much, much lower than those of a female; compare the need to grow and maintain a body that is not significantly larger than a woman's to the costs to her of gestating and breastfeeding a human baby. In these circumstances, Key calculated that it would be worthwhile, in the first instance, for a male to invest some energy and contribute to the care of a female's children, even if they were not his, to try and increase the chance that he would be looked on favourably as the father of her next baby. However, as evolution favours kin selection – preferentially helping those to whom we are genetically related – so a second stage would rapidly evolve where men would begin to 'mate guard' females. This would involve the male spending all of his time in close proximity to the female to ensure that when she next became fertile, a tricky thing to pinpoint in human females, he was there to take full advantage of the opportunity to mate. The downside of this for the male would be that he would remove himself from the mating market and have to move away from a promiscuous, but potentially very productive, mating strategy. This would reduce his lifetime number of offspring and make it even more critical that those he did have survived to maturity to ensure the survival of his genes. As a consequence, he would begin to invest heavily in the children of his mate who, on the upside, he could be sure were his as a consequence of his almost constant presence at her side. Key calculated that the point at which this process occurred in our prehistory – that is, where the costs to the female of reproducing were much higher than those to the male – was, you guessed it, with the emergence of the large-brained but similarly sized *Homo heidelbergensis* half a million years ago.

And this 500,000-year evolutionary story still has relevance for the fathers of today for three main reasons. Firstly, with the first fathers we see the emergence of the two key characteristics that still define the role of the father today, regardless of where he lives. These are protection and teaching. As this book progresses, I will return again and again to the keen need in all fathers to ensure their children's survival and to support their learning, particularly in relation to the complex social world in which our species exists. Secondly, it tells us that human fatherhood is not simply a by-product of the male desire to procreate, but that it was positively selected for by natural selection. Evolution is obsessively efficient, and it will only lead a species down the route of a complex change in behaviour or anatomy if it is really the *only* way to ensure the survival of that species. Human fatherhood could be said to be the epitome of such a change. It was a world-altering change in behaviour with far-reaching consequences for our species, and it would not have been selected for unless it conferred considerable benefits on us. And finally, and perhaps most importantly, this evolutionary story tells us that fathering is innate, not learnt, as we are often led to believe. Yes, you do need to learn all the practical aspects of nappy changing, bathing and feeding, but so does mum. If you have ever seen a new mother struggle as she tries to tackle the skill that is breastfeeding, it is clear that we all need time to learn to be a parent. But your parenting instinct is within you, a lesson I learnt at the very start of my career.

I first studied anthropology under a wonderful primatologist called Simon Bearder. He had made a career studying the tiny, nocturnal bush babies of Africa. In our first lecture, he explained our closeness to our ape and monkey cousins and that, really, we are just a primate with an unusually large brain and an insatiable curiosity, which results in a constant drive to learn and innovate. He explained that in many ways this was a wonderful thing, but sometimes, by constantly trying to be better, we denied our basic instincts and abilities. And one area in which we did this to our detriment was parenting. As two of the dads in my study found, parenting is a steep learning curve and you may slip up initially, but your instinct to father is strong and will ultimately set you on the right path:

Noah: You'll get stuff wrong, but as long as you don't seri-
ously injure them, you just have to . . .
Adrian: Like when she first moved in, maybe four days later
we took her out for a really long walk in her Phil and Ted
buggy, thinking, *Look at our wonderful child* . . . [At one point
we said,] 'She's getting very red, isn't she?!' An hour and a
half later we're thinking, *Have we put enough sunscreen on?*
She was a bit pink! And there was the time we were swing-
ing her in the park and, because we didn't know our own
strength, we kind of swung her right round and we were
waiting to hear shoulders dislocating! So we didn't do that
again, did we?

Noah and Adrian, dads to Judy (seven)

The message is: listen to your instincts. Tune in to your inner
primate, and you will know how to bring up your child. All
parents are different, and they will achieve their parenting
goals in very different ways. But your anatomy, your brain,
your genes, your hormones have all been shaped by evolution to make you a parent. The instinct and ability to parent
is there, you just have to listen for it. And dads, that includes
you too.

For the rest of this book, we will stay firmly in the present.
We will explore how evolution has invested heavily in shaping
men to be fathers – neurologically, genetically, physiologically
and psychologically – and how, by being close to their children, today's fathers garner benefits that are of value not
only to them and their children but also to our wider society.
But the message from our evolutionary past is this: fathers

are not mere adjuncts to mothers, occasional babysitters or bag-carriers. They are the consequence of half a million years of evolution and they remain a vital part of the human story.

PART TWO

Conception and Pregnancy

CHAPTER TWO

Babies on the Brain

Pregnancy, Identity and Embracing the Bump

There is an oft-quoted but ill-founded belief that mothering is instinctive – women are born to want, and are born fully equipped to care for, children. Speaking as the mother of two young daughters, I can assure you it is not instinctive; I will never forget the steep learning curve of first-time motherhood, which made even negotiating cleaning my teeth or emptying the dishwasher while caring for a newborn seem an insurmountable task. However, I did have a head start compared to my husband. Pregnancy, childbirth and breastfeeding are hugely emotional and physical experiences underpinned by a sea of wonderful hormones, which are there to prepare our bodies for motherhood, ease the pain and trauma of birth and motivate us to form quick and deep bonds to our new babies – vital if we are to continue to care for them despite the lack of sleep and constant demands for food. In contrast, fathers have no such experiences to rely upon and it would appear, on the surface at least, that the nine months of pregnancy pass by without much impact on the prospective dad, beyond some stressful visits to IKEA and a bit of elementary cot construction. For fathers, it would seem to be the case that the process of becoming a parent and bonding with his child can only really start once his baby is born.

When does a father become a father? Let's see. It might be at the point he expresses a desire to have a child. Or with the moment of conception. Maybe during pregnancy, when the realization of the need to adopt a new identity dawns. Or it may only commence at the point of birth. In this chapter, I want to explore what happens to a dad during pregnancy. I want to look at his biology, his psychology and his behaviour. To understand how he begins to form the crucial bond with his unborn child, work with his partner to create a parenting team and begin to form his new identity of 'dad'. For many years, it was felt that it was only when he was holding his newborn child in his arms that a man became a father and the relationship with his baby began. Before this point, pregnancy was something that was quite clearly happening to someone else. But would it be so surprising to hear that, with the momentous changes in anatomy and behaviour that were the cause and consequence of the emergence of fatherhood, evolution saw fit to ensure that, even before birth, dads were firmly tied into the family?

Oxytocin is a hormone with a multifaceted role. Produced by a tiny structure at the base of your brain called the pituitary gland, it has several important roles within the body. It is responsible for the commencement of labour, the production of milk and the manufacture and motility of sperm – all vital stages in the journey of reproduction. But it is within your brain that its real power is apparent. For oxytocin is the lubricant that causes many new bonds to form: lover to lover, parent to child, best friend to best friend. It acts a little like alcohol, reducing any inhibitions to forming new partnerships, causing you to walk across the room and strike up conversation with the object of your desire. We all have a baseline level of oxytocin and variations in this level between individuals, caused by both our genes and our environment, mean that we are all different in the extent to which we face down our shyness and plunge into new relationships. And this includes the father–child relationship. We will look at how a man's individual characteristics affect his fathering behaviour, and the ease with which he bonds with his baby, in later chapters.

In addition, oxytocin works closely with another key neurochemical: dopamine. Dopamine is described as a reward chemical and acts in an area of your brain called the reward centre, because its release results in feelings of intense happiness and euphoria. You will be able to imagine what I mean if you recall the pleasure associated with eating chocolate or your favourite takeaway – that's dopamine. Dopamine and oxytocin have a wonderful working relationship, particularly when a new bond is starting to form. Firstly, in combination they work to make the brain more plastic, meaning that it is easier to make changes to its neural structure – vital when you need to form new memories or learn new facts about someone. Secondly, they complement each other really well. I like to describe their relationship as being a little like 'good cop' and 'overenthusiastic cop'. Dopamine – our overenthusiastic cop – acts to give you the vigour and motivation to get off the sofa and form that new relationship. But enthusiasm can sometimes mean that the finer points of relationship formation are missed in the flurry of activity. So, oxytocin – acting to silence our fear circuits and promote our affiliative circuits (which motivate us to form and then maintain our relationships) – dampens the more extreme impacts of dopamine on our ability to concentrate, meaning that you are afforded enough calm headspace to make the relationship work.

For many years, oxytocin was seen as the female love hormone, largely because of its association with birth and breastfeeding, but in recent years it has become clear that it is as crucial to male relationships as female. And it is essential to the formation of the human parenting team. Recent research has shown that fathers and mothers who live together during pregnancy exhibit similar levels of circulating oxytocin within their blood. The team behind this finding is headed by Professor Ruth Feldman, a developmental psychologist from Bar-Ilan University in Israel. Feldman and her team are arguably the most prolific and impactful contributors to our knowledge of the neurochemistry of fatherhood. They are a wonderfully diverse group, and their work on the neurobiology and neurology of fatherhood, together with contributions from the fields of psychology and behavioural science, have led the way in our understanding of what it is to be a dad. But on discovering this amazing synchrony in baseline oxytocin between expectant mums and dads – its sheer ubiquity among couples ruling out the possibility that it is simply a coincidence – even Feldman and her team could not give an absolute explanation of why it existed. They just knew that it had something to say about the fundamental importance of the parenting team to a child. Their many hours of behavioural observation led them to suggest that this neurochemical phenomenon may have something to do with the close parallels in behaviour that we have all observed between two tightly bonded lovers – the common phrases, shared gestures and mirrored body language. They observed that when two people are in a close and supportive relationship, this is often reflected in a mirroring of speech and movement and that this is paralleled by a synchrony in a range of measures – known as physiological markers – such as heart rate, body temperature and blood pressure. They coined the term bio-behavioural synchrony to describe this phenomenon. The team hypothesized that the cause of the synchrony in oxytocin levels in parents-to-be could be explained by taking this observation of behavioural and physiological synchrony one step further, to suggest that this close relationship is underpinned by similar brain activity and hormonal levels, including those hormones that are vital to our long-term relationships. It is as if evolution has acted to ensure that, even before birth, dad and mum are primed to approach the parenting of their baby from the same viewpoint by ensuring they get an equal neurochemical reward. This work, as with so much of the work on fatherhood, is at an early stage, but it does seem that this mechanism could explain the close relationship between oxytocin levels in prospective parents. And this push for synchrony isn't limited to the merely neurobiological. The parents' psychology also undergoes a fundamental transformation.

An individual's personality can be split into five dominant elements, known in the psychological community as the 'big five'. First developed in the 1970s by two research teams, who independently managed to arrive at the same conclusion, and based on the analysis of thousands of personalities, the concept of the big five posits that every personality, regardless of your language or culture, can be boiled down to five essential elements. These five elements are: extraversion (the desire to seek out relationships, stimulation and fun – your classic party animal); openness (a wish to gain new experiences); agreeableness (empathy with others); neuroticism (anxiety and a heightened sense of threat); and conscientiousness (the ability to organize, plan and stick to the rules). All personalities contain these elements to a greater or lesser degree, and it appears, although debate still rages, that your personality is relatively stable for your lifespan. But the practical and behavioural changes that accompany the major upheaval that is new parenthood do appear to cause a degree of beneficial disruption. As with oxytocin levels, parents-to-be who cohabit during pregnancy seem to undergo some change in their personalities to bring them into line with each other.

I am aware from my own studies that dads' personalities undergo a change – once-patient men become less patient fathers and the once-timid can find new confidence in being a dad. But in their study of new and established parents, Sarah Galdiolo and Isabelle Roskam of Université Catholique de Louvain in Belgium found firm evidence that these changes in dad are mirrored in mum. In their long-term study of 204 parental couples, followed from pregnancy to one year after birth, they found that as compared to non-parents, parents saw an alignment in the degree to which their personalities expressed openness, agreeableness and neuroticism. These are all factors that orientate a person to be aware of someone else's life experience and be prepared to accommodate them, and are fundamental to the healthy functioning of the family. By experiencing a degree of synchrony in their personalities, mum and dad were being primed to be empathetic to each other's experience, to be open to the experience of a new baby and alert to threats to the family. Take Nigel's experience as an example:

> There have been times when [my friends] have said, 'Oh, we're going to go out on the Friday night for drinks and stuff, and you're welcome if you want to, but you probably can't, because you have Poppy.' And I find myself thinking, *It's not so much that*. I still want to see my friends and it's not that I can't any more; it's just I'm getting older, I have a kid and I feel responsible for her. It's not that I'm not allowed to, I just don't want Liz to be at home looking after Poppy while I'm out with my friends, just going to pubs, having drinks. It's not a special event. It's something I can do any time, and this is a time I should be at home, because Poppy is changing every day.

> *Nigel, dad to Poppy (six months)*

However, Galdiolo and Roskam found that while mum and dad were in tune regarding these family-orientated aspects of personality, the element that drives them to seek out excitement and reward outside the couple – extraversion – did something different. For mum, this aspect of personality was unaltered by becoming a parent, but for dad there was a significant decline in the extent to which this formed part of his personality. Once they are on the road to parenthood, the personality of a father alters from being one orientated to outside experiences to one that is inward-looking, towards the familiar and comfortable – the family. Nigel's quote above illustrates this change in perspective perfectly. If you are a dad-to-be, then what these fascinating instances of biological and psychological synchrony and asynchrony are telling us is not only that evolution wants you to act as a baby-raising team alongside your partner, but that during pregnancy you are not simply an interested bystander but are being primed biologically and psychologically to contribute fully to that team.

* * *

I built the cot and put the nursery together, put up some shelves . . . it was all me. It's been quite nice, that's my way of contributing. She is busy growing a baby, which I can't do, but I can do the physical stuff here . . .

Tim, expectant dad

Fathers nest. Often, when I ask the fathers I study, like Tim, what they are doing during the pregnancy to prepare for the arrival of their baby, their responses are scattered with anecdotes about painting nurseries, constructing furniture and carrying out extensive research into the best buggy or car seat. Indeed, it is fair to say that buggy shopping seems to get fathers particularly excited, especially if there is scope for a three-wheeled, off-road option. While we may laugh at this sudden flurry of DIY, for the dad-to-be, who may struggle to find a way into the pregnancy, being able to make this contribution helps him to feel involved. But beyond this, many dads also speak of their growing relationship with their baby.

Often, they describe how they sing, talk or even read to the bump, gaining huge joy from any movements the baby makes in response. Many imagine what their future child will look like and what experiences they will enjoy together.

Attachment, a term coined by psychologists to describe the intensely close bond that develops between two people, is fundamental to the parent–infant bond. The father of attachment theory is British child psychiatrist John Bowlby, who began his work in the 1950s. Bowlby rejected previous theories of attachment that posited that the bond between parent and child was motivated by the child's hunger or the requirement for dependency, something that the child should outgrow by adulthood, and argued that it is based upon a deep emotional bond between parent and child that is crucial to the child's healthy development. As such, many mammalian infants, including us, are born with an innate drive to seek out their attachment figure. Much of Bowlby's early work focused exclusively on the mother–infant attachment and positioned it as a behaviour directed from the child to the mother, rather than being two-way. Today, we know that the latter is true – mothers form attachments to their children as well – and that it is also a phenomenon of the father–child relationship. The most common attachment relationships are those between parent and child and between romantic lovers, but they can exist between very close friends and even, some would suggest, pets and owners. Attachment is hard to define – it is one of those phenomena that is difficult to pin down, but psychologists know it when they see it. If we were to observe an attachment relationship – be it romantic, parental or based in deep friendship – we would see two people who crave physical closeness, who constantly monitor each other's emotional reaction to help themselves assess the environment and who become distressed on separation. Think of a puppy separated from its mother or a young child from its parent. We will revisit attachment in Chapter Seven, when we look at the development of the relationship between dad and baby after birth, but here I want to think about the relatively new idea that this bond can begin to form even before birth.

It is beyond debate that a mother forms an attachment to her unborn baby – a process that is given a huge boost by her ability to feel her baby moving and the experience of going on an intensely physical and emotional journey in partnership with her child. This has been referred to as the mothering privilege. But is this really a privilege that only mum can benefit from? There is now a powerful body of evidence to suggest that this privilege can be shared. Dads can feel the same powerful tug of love for their unborn baby, and they have been helped in this in no small way by the advent of the ultrasound scan. With the arrival of this technology, fathers could, for the first time, step beyond their imagination and actually see and hear their baby. Tim's recollection of his first scan makes it clear how powerful this experience can be:

> I think the scan was the first time I began to believe it. Not that I didn't believe it before, but the scan gave me the reassurance that it was real. Knowing for the first time, seeing the evidence on the screen, it was brilliant. Incredible. I was amazed, elated, incredulous.
>
> *Tim, expectant father*

Although it was pioneered in Glasgow during the 1950s, ultrasound use during pregnancy only became routine in the UK during the early 1970s, and it wasn't until the end of that decade that it made an appearance in the United States. So, today's fathers are one of the first generations to routinely be given this opportunity to see their unborn child and, overall, the ability to see one's baby during pregnancy is a positive thing. For the fathers in my studies, whether to attend scans is generally a no-brainer and while there are anxieties surrounding the possibility of discovering issues with the baby, in the majority of cases the overwhelming emotions when baby is finally seen are ones of relief, pride and joy. In these times of rapid innovation, parents can now not only hear and see their baby, but they can get the full surround-sound experience with a 4D scan. These scans show the baby in three dimensions and in real time – that's the fourth dimension. The opportunities for early discussions about who he or she looks like are endless. For fathers, who are largely unaware of the physical exertions of their unborn child, this affords an amazing opportunity to parallel the experiences of the mother. Gone are the days of the grainy black-and-white image, to be replaced by an all-singing, all-dancing movie that can be downloaded to a DVD and taken home with you to view at your pleasure as many times as you like. In a study of the comparative impact of 2D and 4D scanning techniques on prospective parents, Pier Righetti and his colleagues, based in the departments of obstetrics and gynaecology at two Italian hospitals, found that fathers experienced a much greater leap in attachment to their unborn baby following a 4D scan as compared to a 2D scan, even when their attachment was

31

measured two weeks after the appointment. It is possible that the opportunity to view your child moving in three dimensions, combined with the freedom to rewatch them again and again, enables fathers to remain connected to their child throughout the long nine months of pregnancy.

The attachment between parent and child is the first, and arguably most powerful, attachment an individual will form, and whether this is a healthy or unhealthy attachment will mould the baby's health and behaviour for life. As such, the attachment between father and child has long-term implications for the child, family and society as a whole. In recent years, we have come to view the bond between father and child as a different kind of connection, forming a unique and important relationship. Ben's experience makes it clear that this bond begins to form, for both dad and baby, well before birth:

> When my wife was pregnant with Rosie, I would sing 'Twinkle Twinkle, Little Star' to her. When she was born, as soon as she was up on mum's tum, the umbilical cord still attached, I sang 'Twinkle Twinkle, Little Star' and instantly she recognized it, and that was one of those moments that will always be with me.

> *Ben, dad to Rosie (eighteen months)*

Australian psychologist John Condon of Flinders University in Australia has led the field in identifying the important aspects of attachment both before and after birth and, more importantly, in defining the differences between father-to-child and mother-to-child attachment. If you are an expectant dad, whose relationship to your baby-to-be is mostly in your mind, three factors seem to be key in the extent to which you will bond with your unborn child. Firstly, how often you find yourself daydreaming about your baby and the emotions this elicits in you. Particularly key is to what extent you visualize your baby as a 'little person' and to what extent you experience positive, as opposed to negative, feelings towards them. So, are you preoccupied by thoughts about who he or she might resemble and what they might be called, and do such thoughts elicit feelings of tenderness, love and happiness? Or do you rarely picture your baby and, when you do, is your response one of irritation, anger or frustration?

The second factor is how comfortable you are with your chosen identity as a father and, more specifically, to what extent you imagine being an 'involved father'. The term 'involved father' was first coined in the 1980s to describe the type of father who wished to co-parent his child and have as much input into his child's care and emotional and physical development as the mother – it's the 'new dad' of the popular press. This new breed of father was someone who stood in stark contrast to the more traditional image of the breadwinning disciplinarian that epitomized the dads of earlier decades. For one of the fathers in my studies, being an involved dad was his goal:

> My role is to support emotionally and financially. I think it
> is a bit of everything. In parenthood, everything is joint – I
> don't believe that I should be the sole money-earner and
> Julie should be the sole parent; I think we should split it

evenly. Our job is to provide our child with money, emotional support, protection, love, everything. I mean, I think it is an amazing thing to be a dad. You've got such a responsibility ... it just encompasses everything.

Colin, dad to Freya (six months)

The type of father you want to be has a fundamental effect on the nature of the attachment you form to your unborn baby. In their study of attachment and identity, Australian psychologists Cherine Habib and Sandra Lancaster found that expectant dads who included 'father' as a significant component in their identity, alongside husband and worker, for example, and who identified most highly with the role of co-parent had stronger attachment to their unborn child than those who envisaged a primary role as breadwinner. And many men, like Mark, are consciously embracing this identity:

I don't want to be doing sixty hours a week and not [be] there. When I was growing up, my dad was a successful man, a director of a company. But I only remember seeing him at weekends ... I do dinner, I do bath, I do bed ... every single night, and long may that continue ... I want to be here, [to] be remembered.

Mark, dad to Emily (six months)

Pregnancy is one of the few events in life when we *are* able to take some time to prepare for a major change in our circumstances. The other key transitions – puberty, first love, first loss – are a little harder to predict. Parents have the opportunity to take the nine months of pregnancy to prepare practically and emotionally for the new arrival. As is clear from the voices of the dads we have heard so far in this chapter, for many fathers, considering what sort of parent they want to be is an important part of this preparation. And while this consideration of identity is critical to attachment, it is also important to the man's sense of self and his relationship with his partner; all important factors in how effectively a man transitions to being a dad. Here, the power of dad's imagination is key:

> Before I had a child, the dream I had was me with my baby in their room because they are a bit upset, nursing them in a rocking chair. So, before my little girl arrived, I got my mum's rocking chair and put it in her room. When it did happen, I was like, 'At last! I'm in a rocking chair! I've got a baby in my arms!' Like when people dream of a white wedding, that was my dream when I had a baby.
>
> *Adrian, dad to Judy (seven)*

Finally, one external factor has a major influence on how well you will bond with your unborn child, and that is the nature of your relationship with your partner. Where the relationship between parents-to-be is strong and healthy, with high relationship satisfaction and mutual support for each other's roles, fathers tend to form stronger attachments with their unborn babies than those who may feel more at a distance from a partner. Obviously, adding a baby to an established relationship is a tricky journey for any couple to navigate, but the more this journey can be travelled together, the better for the family.

For the majority of fathers, attachment to their unborn baby increases as the pregnancy progresses. However, for some fathers, developing this relationship is not so straightforward. Some men, like Jim, below, may lack an adequate fathering role model, others may struggle with their own mental health, while some dads-to-be may experience discord in their relationship with the birth mother.

> I spent a lot of time before my son was born thinking, *What should I be? What is my role?* My parents divorced when I was quite young, so it was very tough for me because I didn't really have a model set in my mind of what a real father should be ... Mine was this distant, fun guy who came on weekends, but what I want to become is someone who cares about my son and spends time with him. Unlike my father, who didn't get that opportunity.

> *Jim, dad to Sean (six months)*

In cases such as these, the ability to assess the strength of a father's attachment before birth can help in diagnosing future problems in that relationship, which in turn has wider ramifications for society as a whole. As you will see in Chapter Ten, as a father, your relationship with your child has the potential to have a profound influence on their behavioural, emotional and psychological development that is separate to any influence mum may have. Where the attachment is strong, fathers are the promoters of good mental health, the encouragers of independence and the supporters of behavioural and lin-guistic development. But where this relationship is found wanting, the consequences have the potential to negatively influence not only the child and its family but also society at large. Children who form insecure attachments to their parents are at an increased risk of developing antisocial behaviours, experiencing addiction and suffering from poor mental health. John Condon's work on antenatal attachment found that, combined with the quality of the relationship between mum and dad, the nature of the father's attachment to his unborn child is the strongest predictor of how well he will relate to his child when it is born. This is an incredibly powerful finding, for it means that we now have a tool that will help us to identify, even before birth, those relationships that may need help.

* * *

Much of the prenatal bond between father and child is down to the dad's imagination and hard work; picturing your child and future relationship, seeking opportunities where you can to interact with your partner's baby bump and taking the time to consider the sort of dad you want to be. Take Tim:

> I hope I'm starting to build a relationship with the baby . . . It is hard, it feels like you're talking to this thing that has no idea what you are or what you're doing. But I talk to it quite a lot, I touch it quite a lot. I like to be involved if I am here.

We had a great game of high five a few days ago, where I was patting and it was patting back … It could have just been hiccupping, but it was great, really cool.

Tim, expectant dad

We know that the bonding neurochemicals that epitomize pregnancy and childbirth – oxytocin and dopamine – *are* available to dad, but at a much lower intensity and after a lot more time and work (childbirth aside!). But evolution has not abandoned dads entirely to a pregnancy powered by the imagination – it has one more wonderful trick up its sleeve to help fathers make the transition to fatherhood.

Many would say that testosterone is the hormone that makes a man a man. Its release within the womb at between six to twelve weeks' gestation leads to the development of the penis and testes in a male baby and influences the development of the brain. Once born, many argue that it is testosterone and its influence on brain development and behaviour that drives male children to select male-gendered toys to play with and turn every stick into a sword or gun. During puberty, it controls the distribution of fat and muscle and the development of bones that sees the jaw, shoulders and chest widen and strengthen and promotes the growth of hair on the chest, face and genitals. And it is the hormone that decides how effective you will be as a lover and a father.

It has long been understood that men who have higher circulating testosterone are more successful at attracting mates. This may be as a result of two things: a stronger testosterone-driven motivation to seek out women and a preference in women for partners with strong jaws and chests – the better to protect and provide. However, when a man decides to stick with one woman and settle down, his previously beneficially high levels of testosterone suddenly become a hindrance. While he tries to focus on his new role of committed partner and father, his hormones are driving him to keep looking for another mate, something that would be detrimental to any offspring who require his care. This is known as the 'challenge hypothesis' and it certainly is a challenge. First developed by British zoologist John Wingfield, the challenge hypothesis tries to tackle the thorny question of how a man can balance the need to be a successful lover before having children with the need to be a successful parent after. And the answer? That testosterone has got to go.

And it does. Across cultures as diverse as polygynous Senegalese agriculturalists, middle-class Israelis, high-investing Filipino fathers, middle-class Canadians, non-cohabiting Jamaican fathers and my own group of UK dads, fathers have significantly lower testosterone levels than non-fathers, regardless of whether they live with their children or not. And we know that men with lower levels of testosterone are more responsive to a child's cry, are more likely to wish to co-parent their child and show more empathy and affection towards their children than men with higher testosterone levels. Testosterone makes a considerable contribution to differences between individuals in fathering behaviour. We'll dig into this a bit more in Chapter Six. But the question arises: is it simply men with generally lower circulating testosterone who become fathers, hence globally dads have lower testosterone than non-dads, or does becoming a father somehow suppress testosterone levels?

Lee Gettler of Northwestern University, Illinois, has the answer. In a groundbreaking five-year study, Gettler and his colleagues followed a group of Filipino men as they embarked upon relationships and fatherhood. Meeting them first as single men, they measured their baseline levels of testosterone. Five years later, they visited the men again. Of the 624 men tested at the start of the study, 162 had become first-time fathers during the five-year period. Not only were these 162 men the individuals who had exhibited the highest testosterone at the start of the study, but five years later they now exhibited the lowest levels. The men who had remained single and those who had found partners but not become fathers saw no real change in their testosterone levels. Gettler had his answer. Men who have high circulating testosterone levels *are* more success-ful at finding mates *and* they see the largest drop in testosterone when they become fathers. Testosterone levels are suppressed by becoming a father and, it would appear, while rising slightly following the end of the first few newborn weeks, they never reach their pre-fatherhood levels again. Evolution has selected for a mechanism that allows men to successfully balance the opposing needs of the single man and the devoted father.

* * *

Um, I think I've changed. I hope I have. I've learnt to be a lot calmer with things. I feel there is more of a purpose in my life now. I feel a lot happier. I mean, in theory we should be more like, 'Oh my god, what have we done?', because having three of them has been tough, but we have been really lucky.

Matt, dad to Tom (seven), Sam (three) and James (seven months)

I always start my study of new fathers during pregnancy, and one of the early questions they encounter is what they think the impact of having a baby will be on their lives. This is generally something to which they have given some thought, and the majority are not unrealistic about the potential for major upheaval that their impending situation will bring. Many recognize the effect parenthood will have upon their home and social life; altering everyday practicalities, causing the relationship with their partner to change and putting an extra financial burden on the family.

But for some men, like Colin, anxiety lies in the question of whether they are capable of stepping up to the job. Indeed, whether they have the requisite qualifications.

I think setting an example worries me, because I always want to be successful and [to] be seen as successful by people around me – family and friends – and I always want [my daughter] to see me that way. So, I don't want to be seen as a failure and I don't want her to grow up as a failure, almost. I want to make sure I've done a good job raising her and that people can see I've done a good job raising her.

Colin, dad to Freya (six months)

In one of the first studies of its kind, sociologist Tina Miller of Oxford Brookes University followed a group of new fathers as they transitioned to fatherhood. One of her subjects reflected upon how no one assesses your suitability to be a dad: 'You get selected to do your job on a skill base or your character . . . Father, you can become a father quite easily, it's frightening how easy it is . . . You know, am I up to it? Will I be able to cope with it? I don't know.' But in my experience of new fathers, such thoughts are fleeting and rather than being a source of ongoing anxiety, it is an opportunity to redefine who they are; to adopt a new role, identity or perspective. Many of the fathers in my studies have found that becoming a dad motivates them to 'up their game', acting as an impetus to improve, to ensure they are a good role model for their child, even though their desire to be perfect can lead them to fall short of the high standards they set themselves at times. But while there are downsides to this self-imposed pressure, these are counterbalanced by the benefits that being a father can have for a man's self-esteem and confidence. I can truly say that for the vast majority of the fathers I work with, becoming a dad feels like they have finally found their calling.

Even men who we might imagine would find it difficult to handle the transition to fatherhood – for example, young fathers or those who have not had a suitable role model – can find that becoming a father allows them to reject the stereotype of the authoritarian or absent father, or the example that their father did, or did not, set them, and turn instead to a different model, allowing them to recast themselves and escape their past.

In recent years, sociologists and social anthropologists, who concern themselves with the study of individual societies and cultures, have begun to explore beyond the negative tabloid headlines that label all young fathers as irresponsible and lazy, to try to understand whether positive stories of young fatherhood exist; an undertaking I fully support. What they found is that some young fathers *are* beginning to turn the narrative of the disinterested or absent teenage father on its head and are finding salvation and transformation in being a dad. Fathers who, in the past, would have felt the need to live up to the tough-guy image promoted by their societies are using the opportunities afforded by new fatherhood to reject this life path. For example, population scientists from the London School of Hygiene and Tropical Medicine and the University of KwaZulu-Natal found that in South Africa, where the overriding image of black manhood is one of dominance, oppression and absence, young black fathers are promoting a new idea of fatherhood where real men reject womanizing, drug-taking and irresponsible spending and replace them with a drive to provide money, protection and care for their families. In America, midwife Dr Jenny Foster of the University of Massachusetts found that the possible judgement from their children drove young Puerto Rican fathers to reject the gangland life – and the associated risk of early death or incarceration – to ensure that they were on hand throughout their children's lives to provide care and support and be that all-important role model. For these young fathers, the transition to being a dad truly revolutionized their lives and their futures. From gang member to involved father.

But perhaps one of the groups of fathers for which the change in identity is the most extreme is gay fathers, like Simon:

> Growing up as gay in the time that I did it, [becoming a dad] was never, ever an option for me and that was a really hard part of coming out. I would never be a dad and never have children. And obviously I accepted that. And in my twenties, it was totally fine. That was the way it was going to be. Obviously, as the world has changed ... Then we met and very quickly got together, [and] we felt it was very right. We are lucky in lots of ways. A nice house and money ... So it just all absolutely fits that it would work for us to be dads.

> *Simon, dad to Daisy (six) and Bill (five)*

Until very recently, the prospect of becoming a father was remote for the majority of gay men. The attitude of society to gay adoption and the limit on access to assisted fertility, combined with the erroneous belief that children were best raised in the bosom of the heterosexual nuclear family, meant that, for many men, realizing their sexuality meant coming to terms with never being a parent. However, in some countries, as attitudes have changed and hurdles have been removed, it is now a very real possibility for gay men to become parents – having originally abandoned the fathering identity, they need to pick it back up, dust it off and assume it. Adrian's journey is typical:

I have always wanted children. I remember telling my friend when I was fourteen or fifteen that I was gay [and that] the biggest issue for me was, 'Oh god, gay people don't have children.' That was always a big black cloud over my head. And then, as you get older, you realize that it is a possibility, actually. So, I have always had a very strong pull towards being a parent. I think . . . early on it was a bit like, 'I can't leave this earth without another part of me on it! I can't just die out!' But now that is not part of it.

Adrian, dad to Judy (seven)

For the gay fathers I have worked with, adopting the 'dad' identity was sometimes difficult, as there are few examples or models of gay parenting to follow and many find it difficult to reconcile their identity with that of the overtly heterosexual persona of the father. Combined with this, announcing to the world that you are going to be a parent does not necessarily come with the overwhelmingly positive response that heterosexual couples have come to expect.

But the gay father does have one massive advantage in the identity stakes, as compared to a heterosexual man: his role is less bound by gender. In the heterosexual relationship, society has decreed there is a mother and a father and these roles, and all that society associates with them, are defined by gender. But in the gay parenting relationship, roles are much more fluid, and the part someone plays can be decided based on what someone is good at or prefers, rather than gender. Within the UK, the number of gay fathers is still very small but those who I have interviewed have used this flexibility to construct their own roles. For Simon and his husband Calum, this has meant following a traditional heterosexual model, where Calum is the main full-time wage-earner and Simon has enthusiastically adopted, in his words, the 'mum's role':

> I feel like – obviously, it is all culture and gender stuff, but – I feel like a mum because I am the stay-at-homer. And I pick them up, and they come to me in the night. I am the one they usually come to for nurture and comfort and every little thing. I feel like a mum.

> *Simon, dad to Daisy (six) and Bill (five)*

In contrast, Adrian and Noah have exploited the freedom of their non-gendered situation to be true co-parents, unaffected by any cultural norms regarding the division of labour or the promotion of mum as the primary parent.

> We have gone through the process together. We brought her home ... and we got settled on our own. It was very much us together on a level, getting to know that baby. It wasn't like, 'Oh, you have had nine months of bonding with her in your belly and I feel a bit on the outside.'

> *Adrian, dad to Judy (seven)*

For the modern gay Western father, the flexibility afforded by the newness of gay parenting can make becoming an involved dad considerably easier. Without centuries of culture and tradition, gay fathers can define their role anew.

* * *

It is an undeniable fact that becoming a father changes you. But these changes begin long before you get to hold your newborn in your arms. As your partner's pregnancy progresses, evolution has seen to it that your hormone levels synchronize with those of your partner and your personalities align; and as you touch, talk and sing to the bump, the powerful bonding hormones oxytocin and dopamine begin their job of motivating you to form an attachment to your unborn child – a job made much easier by your powerful imagination. Just before birth, your testosterone level falls and your personality alters, your drive to be extraverted, to look outside the family for stimulation, declines and your openness to new experiences and close social interactions increases. You are being primed to father and to do so from within a team with your partner – a team that has shared goals and a shared vision about what they want their family to be. You are being prepared to become a dad.

And the real-world implications of all this science are these: if you are sitting out the nine months of pregnancy, then there is an opportunity to be seized. The work you put into bonding with your baby now will see you reap the rewards a thousand-fold once your baby is born. So however silly it may feel, try and have a conversation with the bump; talk to it, sing to it, touch it. Read it the complete works of Chaucer if that is your thing, just let it hear your voice. Try to imagine who is in there. What will they be like, look like? What will you do together and what sort of father will you be? Take the time now to have a conversation, uninterrupted by the demands of a newborn, with your partner, your family and friends about what life post-baby will be like and how you might fit into it. It is normal to be worried about the changes that are coming, but if worry becomes anxiety then talk about your thoughts and fears to those closest to you, or the health and social care professionals who *are* there to support you, or seek out the anonymous support of an online forum. There is a list of helpful links at the end of this book. Remember that looking after yourself now means that you will be fully available once your baby is here to dedicate yourself to your new role, your new family and your new life.

CHAPTER THREE

The Importance of Being Dad

It's Not Just About Biology

The Nāyar are a high-ranking caste from the Kerala region of India. Before puberty, a girl is married to an older man of the same or higher caste and then swiftly divorced. When the girl reaches childbearing age, she takes a number of lovers, any of whom could be the biological fathers of her children. However, while the girl designates these men as 'visiting husbands', the men regard the relationship as little more than that of concubine and client. As a consequence, they accept no responsibility for their progeny and, to ensure legitimacy, the children are deemed by the family to be those of the ex-husband. However, as he made for the hills long ago, a male relative of the woman – usually her mother's brother – accepts the position of 'social father' and takes on the role of teacher and protector. What could possibly explain this – to Western eyes, very unusual – arrangement?

The Nāyar are matrilineal. That is, power and inheritance travel down the female line, albeit still in the hands of the matriline's male members. Being a high-ranking caste, the Nāyar are concerned that their position is not diminished by the haemorrhaging of wealth and power to another lineage, as represented by the biological father's family. So, their society has devised this wonderful system that ensures biological dad provides his genes and is then removed from the picture, and that all children – themselves a valuable asset to the family due to future marriage endowments and labour – remain within the control of the matriline but still have a vital father figure in their lives.

Fathers are an essential component of all human cultures. By this I am not referring to their role in reproduction – you don't need a book to tell you they are essential for the creation of human life – but their role within the family and wider society. Within the West, we privilege the position of the bio-logical father and find it difficult to comprehend anyone else occupying this special role. But unlike mothers, whose role is largely dictated by the strictures of their biology – they are necessary to at least carry the developing baby, if not feed it – the identity of the best person to step into the fathering role is considerably more fluid. This means that in many societies the role of the father is not necessarily tied to biological related-ness, nor is it necessarily limited to one man. It is the multiple influences of history, ideology, culture and law mixed with the evolutionary imperative to ensure the survival of one's genes that defines who the father is. The result of this rather complicated combination of factors is that the role of the father is wonderfully diverse around the globe.

In this chapter, I want to take a tour of the world's fathers, to learn who gets to carry the coveted title of 'dad'. You may ask why the lives of fathers around the world should matter to us in the West. Wouldn't our time be better spent supervising homework, cleaning the fridge or catching up on that boxset rather than taking on board the experiences of men in some remote tribe in the Congo? Be assured, your time will be well spent. There are two reasons why our paternal cousins should be of interest to us. Firstly, fatherhood in the West is not the monolithic behaviour that we at first believe it to be. Yes, we have absorbed the nuclear family message and now picture it as our norm, but there have always been significant exceptions to this norm – look at step- and adoptive families. And as societies become more liberal and assisted fertility techniques ever more advanced, who answers to the name 'dad' is becoming ever more diverse. As a consequence, there is much that fathers from other cultures can teach us both in attitude and behaviour. Secondly, it is to provide reassurance. In many cultures, our obsession with biological relatedness would provoke profound confusion. In these societies, dad is the guy who steps up and gets the job done, and whether or not he has a genetic relationship with the child is really of little consequence. If you fulfil the role of the father, then you get the name and the valuable recognition of your society. For the increasing number of men who may not have a biological link to their child, I hope that these lessons from your fellow 'social' fathers are of help.

Over the millennia that have passed since human fatherhood evolved, our ancestors have had to endure many changes in their environment and fortunes that have threatened their survival. They have battled with sabre-toothed cats, endured extremes of temperature change as ice ages swept across the globe, travelled across unexplored and inhospitable lands and battled for supremacy with competing species of hominin. This placed immense pressure on ancestral parents as they fought to protect their children from these new climatic, predatory and environmental threats. Our ancestors survived, and humans have thrived, because we were able to respond to these threats by adapting our behaviour, our culture and, uniquely, our environment. Indeed, we are still doing so today, and because mum is bound up in the energetic exertions of pregnancy and childbirth, it is the father's behaviour that must change swiftly to adapt to these challenges and ensure the survival of his family. And at times this can mean that the best man to be 'dad' is not necessarily the one who was there at conception.

Consider the Western father living in the UK, Europe or North America today. If he is typical, he will be keen to be as involved with his children as is possible, his goal the status of true co-parent. He wants to be there to support, teach, nurture and practically care for his child alongside his partner. But why has he chosen this role? Maybe he has adopted it for a personal reason, because he wants to actively reject the more distant parenting of his father. Or because he has been strongly influenced by the constant media focus on the celebrity dad; the David Beckhams and Brad Pitts of this world seem capable of balancing considerable professional success with model good looks and impeccable fathering skills. It is certainly the case that this move towards co-parenting is due in part to a change in society's beliefs about fathering, driven by a growing understanding of the key influence fathers have on their children's development. But this is far from being the whole story. Colin's experience might give you a hint:

> I had two weeks' paternity leave and I think you should get a lot more than that, because it doesn't just stop after two weeks. Your partner still needs your help, your baby still needs your help as well, so I think men should have more time off work for paternity leave ... Because Julie had a spinal leak, we had a tough time and I was thrown in at the deep end for two weeks because she couldn't do very much, so I was doing everything and then, when I went back to work, she was thrown in at the deep end and I was like, 'Where's my child?' I was used to doing everything and she wasn't there.
>
> *Colin, dad to Freya (six months)*

When my mother gave birth to me in the 1970s, it was usual for a mother to remain in hospital for at least a week after birth, regardless of how straightforward her experience had been. A high midwife-to-mother ratio meant that she would be fully supported in learning to breastfeed and care for her newborn, and her baby would be taken to the nursery every night to enable her to build up her sleep reserves before returning home. Today, the picture is very different. In the UK, a straightforward birth often results in mum and baby being discharged on the same day as delivery. Not for them the gentle introduction to motherhood. Due to the need to move for work, many of us now don't live near our parents and extended family, meaning they are not available to fill the void left by the absence of midwife care. As a result, the only person who can step in and help care for the baby while mum is recovering is dad. Can you hear an echo from 500,000 years ago? Dad has again had to rely on the potential for flexibility in his role to meet the needs of his new family, to step into the breach and ensure his child survives and thrives.

Survival really is the key focus for fathers, and we will talk about how this is achieved throughout a child's life later on. But at the very basic level, a parent's job is to focus on the survival of their genes from the moment of conception, and human fathers are no different. In the West, it is generally the biological dad who steps up when such survival is threatened, but in other countries the very real risk that the biological father may not survive to see his children grow has led to a very different solution to the fathering conundrum.

The Aché of Paraguay in South America are distinguished in the anthropological world by two main characteristics. Firstly, they are a hugely violent society who are almost permanently at war with their neighbours. Secondly, they exhibit a relatively rare form of fathering that results in children having more than one dad. Relatively common in South America but absent elsewhere, this method of parenting means that a child doesn't just have a single biological dad but has a number of 'social' fathers as well. A social father is one who takes on the role of the father, and everything that implies, in a child's life, but isn't involved in the act of conception. So, he can be genetically related – say, mum or dad's brother or uncle – but is not the biological father. Within the Aché society, both men and women are encouraged to be promiscuous, and it is often the case that a woman will sleep with all the brothers of a single family, among many others. Importantly, the Aché do not believe that conception is a single event, but one that lasts for a significant period before a child is born. For them, the biological father is the man who had sex with the mother the closest to the point at which she stopped having periods – or the point at which they recognize that 'the blood has ceased to flow'. However, *every* man who has had sex with the mother in the *year* before the child is born is also deemed to be a father. Adults within the community will distinguish between all these different men so they know how the land lies – it's rather like keeping track of a very complicated scenario in a daytime soap – but significantly the child will refer to them all by the same term. The labels different men adopt indicate their role in the process of conception – the *miare* is the 'one who put it in' (our biological dad), the *peroare* the 'one who mixed it', the *momboare* the 'one who spilled it out' and the *bykuare* the 'one who provided its essence'. It is a truly collaborative act. Initially, the man identified as the biological father (the *miare*) will be expected to adopt the role of the primary father, although how this role plays out is very different from the West. Not for him the focus on care and emotional engagement that characterizes the modern Western father. Rather, the overriding responsibility for this dad is to prevent his family being killed in the frequent intertribal raids that blight his village. The consequence of such a role choice is that he is at significant risk of dying and leaving his children fatherless.

The rate of mortality among Aché men is astonishingly high, and children who do not have a father are left unprotected and at a significant risk of being killed by invading tribes.

Conquering males do not want the burden of raising another man's child and infanticide is common. It is with this very real threat of death that the need for more than one father becomes clear. For it is with the death of the primary father that the secondary or social fathers step up to take on the fathering role and protect the children. Research by social anthropologists Kim Hill and Magdalena Hurtado – who spent many years living alongside the Aché – found that children who have secondary fathers have an 85 per cent chance of survival, compared to only 70 per cent for those children who simply have a single dad. This is a significant difference. On average children will have two fathers, but it is not unknown for a single child to have ten. So, the Aché do not have an ideological belief in free love, but rather their focus on promiscuity is a pragmatic survival tactic. By confusing paternity, men are encouraged to protect the tribe's children on the off chance that they are the biological father. And the man who has the most potential for being the *real* biological father puts up with sharing his partner with many men – an act apparently in direct opposition to the evolutionary drive to ensure paternity – because in a war-torn world it gives his genes the best chance of survival.

So, the biological dad is but one solution to the need for a father in a child's life. While not many societies follow the Aché's lead and extol the virtues of multiple fathers, many do follow traditions that mean the single father of a child is as likely to be a social father as a biological one. And in these societies, and many others like them, a biological father will step aside – willingly or by force – because it is for the good of his child and, ultimately, his genes. So, the biological dads of the Nāyar tribe are content to see their role given to someone else because they know that, in this strongly matriarchal society, their children will have a better chance of survival and success within their mother's family than within their own. They will give up the opportunity to be involved in their children's lives and cede their role to the children's maternal uncles because they know that, by doing this, their children will have access to all the financial and political resources necessary to ensure their success in the deeply stratified world of Indian society.

The fathering practices of the Nāyar and Aché encompass the idea that a father can be many things, even many people, during a child's lifetime. Ultimately, what is important is not biological relatedness, rather that a father figure is present to ensure the child's survival. But such practices are not solely the preserve of distant tribes.

We are as likely to find a social father in the West as we are within the forests of Paraguay or the expanses of India – we simply call them by a different name. If you were to ask a South African child to reflect on their father, what would quickly become apparent is that while they talk repeatedly about their father being present, being there for them, they are not necessarily referring to their biological father. In their study of black South African fathers, Kopano Ratele, Tamara Shefer and Lindsay Clowes of the University of the Western Cape report that adult children had a very clear picture of who a father was, but it was not bound by biological relatedness or the Western concept of the nuclear family. The extended family is key. Indeed, it is the tradition that biological fathers are more often than not absent for long periods from the family home, fulfilling their role as breadwinner; caring and nurturing the child and being a role model and teacher is the responsibility of the grandfathers, uncles and male members of the community. This is not a short-term solution to a short-lived jobs shortage but the norm – when today's fathers become grandfathers, they will in turn assist their sons by raising their grandchildren. And for the children of these families, such an arrangement is often seen as ideal – they have the support of a whole raft of players whose importance may grow or recede depending upon the child's changing needs. For many, this is an advantage as compared to depending solely on a single biological father, as different fathers bring different skills to the table. In recent years, much has been said about the crisis of family within South Africa, a crisis that is driven in part, many argue, by a culture of absent biological fathers. But as Ratele and her colleagues put it, if we step outside our restricted concept of the father and family for one minute, we can see that many South African children do have a father present. In fact, they have a whole team.

In many cases, the non-nuclear family arrangements highlighted by these non-Western and newly industrialized examples are centuries old and are of interest precisely because they sit in stark contrast to our focus on biological parenting in the West. However, today in the UK a father may not be genetically related to his child for several reasons, including as a consequence of infertility, leading to the need for donor sperm, or because he has adopted his child or because he makes up one half of a gay couple who want to become fathers. The child of a lesbian couple who have chosen to co-parent with a gay sperm donor and his partner may have both a biological mother and father *and* a social mother and father.

It is wonderful that changes in science and society have enabled men who in the past couldn't conceive of being fathers to fulfil long-held dreams to parent and become dads. But while all fathers can experience the transition to fatherhood as a journey beset by a myriad number of challenges and delights, for social fathers an additional challenge presents itself – how to assert their identity as a dad in a society that is still determined to champion the supremacy of the biological father above all others.

Before 2005, children born via donor insemination (DI) in the UK were not entitled to know anything about the identity of their biological father, and all donations made to sperm banks were anonymized. Authorities conceived of this rule because it was felt that the absolute priority throughout this process of assisted fertility must be to protect the integrity of the nuclear family and the man's role as father at its head. It is not an exaggeration to state that the belief was that society was founded on the bedrock of the nuclear family, and allowing the identity of the donor to be known would undermine the position of the social father within the family. If the possibility were to exist that the sperm donor may materialize and move from the abstract to the real at some point in the future, then the functioning of the family would be continually compromised by the threatening presence of this shadowy 'third parent'. Fathers of children born by DI would know that their child or children were not biologically related to them, but they could come to terms with this reality in the knowledge that they were the sole identifiable father figure and, if they chose, present this scenario to both their child and the wider world. However, with the increase in understanding of genetic inheritance and the acknowledgement that children born by DI have the right to know what their genes may have in store for them, particularly with respect to congenital illness, the law was changed whereby any child born by DI after 1 April 2005 has the right to access information about their biological father at the age of eighteen.

Such a change in the law has meant that both the individual and society have had to grapple with the fact that the role of the father may not rest with one man but be split between the absent biogenetic father and the nurturing, and present, social father. Other societies may have embraced, and extended, this idea long ago, but for us in the West, required to dismantle centuries of ideology regarding the nuclear family, such a change in outlook has not necessarily come easily. At the level of the family, the fathers of DI children, who must confront this challenge on a daily basis, have tackled this new reality in a range of ways. In their study of the fathers of DI children in New Zealand, associate professor Victoria Grace and her colleagues from the Department of Gender Studies at Canterbury University encountered a considerable ambivalence with respect to the donor. On the one hand, fathers were grateful for the donor's altruistic act, but on the other their continued presence led them to be characterized as a threat. For many fathers, the route out of this tension was to deny the existence of the donor, minimize his contribution or to make only jokey or light-hearted reference to his existence. Grace quotes one father as saying, 'He's donated sperm, end of connection', while another comments, 'There is no face, there is no personality that goes along with the donor.'

However, issues do arise when the inevitable discussions

about similarity begin. All parents delight in discussions about where their children have inherited their impressive, quirky or downright annoying traits from and, where one of the cohabiting parents *is* biologically related to the child, such discussions cannot be avoided. For the social fathers in these families, these discussions can be an unwelcome reminder that their partners, male or female, have a genetic connection to their child while they do not. For heterosexual couples, this is a genetic connection that the mother shares with another man. Some families tackle this issue by emphasizing those behaviours that the child has learnt from their social father – the turns of phrase or mannerisms – while others openly acknowledge that the child has gained skills or traits from a third, absent parent, often when the child shows an interest or aptitude for something for which neither parent has ever shown a talent. Indeed, for some couples, the oft-repeated belief that many sperm donors are hard-up medical students is seen as a positive benefit, increasing the chance of conceiving a clever child. For many couples, a focus on trying to find a donor who shares physical traits with the social father is an attempt to align the child with the non-biological father as closely as is possible in the circumstances – to allow for the suggestion that a genetic relationship *does* exist between father and child. Social scientist Lucy Frith's study of non-biological parents in the US found that, beyond ensuring good health, non-biological lesbian mothers identified the donor's interests as key to their selection, while non-biological fathers prioritized the physical attributes of colouring, build and height. This stark sex difference is perhaps understandable if one considers that while the non-biological social mother cannot hide her lack of genetic relatedness to her child, the non-biological father has the option of attempting to blur the boundaries by aligning himself physically with the child.

The complex thought processes that the fathers of DI children have to go through to become comfortable with their role as a social rather than biological father is in part because of our discomfort as a society with the idea of splitting the role across two or more individuals. Among the Aché, the Nāyar and the contemporary population of South Africa, the idea of dispersed fatherhood – multiple, social or both – is supported by society as entirely normal, but within the West we do not provide social fathers with such affirmation. It is probably a consequence of individual personality and experience combined with the wishes and opinions of the wider family that determines how a social father in the West navigates his role. At one extreme, fathers are happy to acknowledge the donor and the contribution he has made to the family while, at the other, some dads find acknowledging that someone else had a role in their child's conception difficult to accept, to the extent that a couple may take the decision not to tell their children about the nature of their conception and deny them full knowledge regarding their origins. Fathers in the latter position often worry that by allowing their child to know their conception story, they may no longer view their social father as their parent or, should biological and social father meet, such a meeting would impact upon the social father's security in his role as a father in a negative way. Whatever the decision regarding disclosure, it is an undeniable fact that navigating the role of social father in the West, often working against the zeitgeist, is an emotionally and psychologically complex task for which social fathers deserve our empathy, acknowledgement and support.

In heterosexual couples where artificial insemination has been used, biological and social father exist at a physical distance from each other. However, in gay couples the possibility exists for social and biological dad to live side by side. Further, the fact that only one man can be the biological father of the child means that the act of becoming a gay father is considerably less spontaneous than it is for the vast majority of heterosexual men – there are many choices to be negotiated and decisions to be made. Not only does a suitable surrogate need to be identified – does one employ an agency surrogate or make an informal arrangement with a female friend or lesbian couple? – but the discussion has to occur regarding paternity – will a conscious decision be taken as to who is to be the biological and who the social father, or will the possibility of actively confusing paternity be considered? In her study of gay fathers, Australian social scientist Deborah Dempsey reports several ingenious ways of allowing both fathers to have an equal shot at being the biological dad: couples have employed artificial insemination with mixed sperm; IVF where both men have their sperm injected into separate eggs and both eggs are implanted into the surrogate; and alternating the role of donor each month until the surrogate becomes pregnant. By utilizing these techniques that blur paternity, gay fathers are moving some way towards mirroring the process of heterosexual conception, where the biological material of both parents contributes to the conception of a baby. However, going to these lengths to confuse the identity of the biological father emphasizes that for some gay parents being the biological parent is still seen as the ultimate prize, with the social father being regarded as very much the secondary role. Where it is clear which of the parents is the social father, many gay fathers go to great lengths to ensure that the parenting scales are 'rebalanced'. In some cases, the social father is listed as the legal father on the birth certificate, while in many cases, even though the couple are aware of the identity of the biological father and the social father, they work hard to keep this information within the couple, even to the extent of not telling the child, to ensure that they are treated equally within the family.

The fact that gay men have to go outside their partnership to become parents means that the families they create always exist outside the traditional stereotype of mum, dad, 2.4 kids and a Labrador with which our society has been historically more familiar. They are always challenging our assumption that a biological dad is somehow different, superior, to a social dad. Writing in the *Journal of Homosexuality*, Tor Folger from the University of Bergen in Norway described a family that consisted of five adults and two children. It consisted of a lesbian couple, one of whom was the biological mother, a gay couple, both of whom were social fathers, and a known biological father who did not have any input into the children's lives but whom the children knew of and could visit if they so desired. Tor's study subject, Bard, and his partner had chosen not to be biologically involved in the act of conception because they were concerned that this would introduce imbalance into their relationship. By using a sperm donor, their standing within the family was equal; they were both social fathers to their two children. Interestingly, once their child was born their views changed starkly as they realized that the relationship with their children was based on presence and involvement rather than mere genetics; their previous obsession with the standing of the biological father evaporated.

> I never believed blood was thicker than water. I [thought if] I had children, I would adopt. I was quite firm about that in my mind, because I just thought there are enough children in the world. I have never believed that a child has to have your blood ... [M]y family is horrific and I thought, *I'm amazing, [even though] they are horrible, so [blood] doesn't really matter!*
>
> Noah, dad to Judy (seven)

The loosening of adoption laws in some countries, enabling gay couples to adopt, has meant there is an increasing number of families in the world whose parenting team does consist of two social fathers. In the US, current figures estimate that 65,500 children had been adopted by gay or lesbian couples by 2015 and the number of gay couples raising adopted children rose from 5 per cent in 1990 to 20 per cent in 2000, a quite colossal and swift increase. Within the UK, since records began in 2006, 2,317 children have been adopted by lesbian, gay or bisexual couples. For the gay fathers I have studied, the decision to adopt has been driven by the belief that genetic relatedness does not trump a relationship based on nurture, care and love, and that the number of children awaiting adoption in the UK makes choosing this route, rather than surrogacy, a bit of a no-brainer; why produce more children when there are so many who need a loving home? Adoption is not an easy route – within the UK, it involves being willing to bare your life and soul to intense scrutiny, attending courses, completing self-reflective and practical assignments and providing evidence that you are a 'kid' person. All this before there is even a suitable child anywhere on the horizon, and knowing that you will soon have to start answering the frequently asked question about how your child copes with being raised without the (assumed) practical, steadying hand of a mum. But with all these added challenges and questions, for the adoptive gay fathers I have interviewed, it is the most wonderful and rewarding of experiences. And that's without a single gene in sight.

> *Adrian*: I mean, our neighbours do it. 'Oh, you have done an amazing job.' And I know they mean she's a great girl, but there is always this edge of 'for two men'.
> *Noah*: It is totally patronizing, and you get that a lot. You get a lot of questions; you get a lot of ... 'Who does what?' And 'who does ...?'
> *Adrian*: 'Who got the mum role?'
> *Noah*: Yeah, 'who got the mum role?' And Judy gets questioned as well.
> *Adrian*: And some people are a bit like, 'Because we know you two men, we thought you would get her and just stick her in a cupboard and hope she grew ...' But actually, we have had some ideas about how to raise a child.
> *Noah*: And we have absolutely loved it. It is the best thing we ever did.

> *Noah and Adrian, dads to Judy (seven)*

As this book progresses, I hope you will come to understand the many roles a father can play, the myriad influences he is under as he shapes his role and how vital he is in creating a world in which his child can live, grow and thrive. I hope that if you are reading this as a social father, your experience chimes with those of the fathers I have described here. That, while you may have concerns regarding your lack of genetic relatedness before your child arrives – concerns you should speak freely about with those who are close to you or who have travelled a similar path – once you have got stuck into the daily tasks and experience of being a dad, these concerns will fade away and you will realize that by *doing* you are a dad. And for many men, the real job of being a dad begins with birth.

PART THREE

Birth

CHAPTER FOUR

A Father Is Born

Dads, Birth, Health and Well-being

A man walks towards a tree, eyes focused firmly on the ground before it. At its base is a pile of firewood. Arranged as a pyramid, the stack of wood is protected by a substantial barrier of thorns. The man crouches by this pile and begins to dig. Once he has dug a small, shallow hole he removes a package wrapped in white linen from his bag. He unwraps the parcel to reveal half a coconut shell. Within the shell is a large, fleshy pink object – a placenta. He places the shell and its contents in the hole and backfills it with soil. Finally, he sets aside the thorns, takes the firewood and builds a fire on top of the shallow grave. He lights it, stands back and watches as the individual sticks catch light and the flames grow. He will leave the fire to burn for a while, but will return regularly night and day to tend to it and ensure it never goes out. After five days he will return, remove the embers and dig the coconut shell and its contents back up. This he will rebury in a site he has selected on the corner of his street, close to his home. He is a new father and the placenta is that of his newborn son.

This man is a contemporary Thai Malay from the beautiful coastal region of Satun, in the south-west of the country. The Satun people believe that the placenta is the same-sex sibling of their baby and, as such, its destiny is intertwined with that of the living child. By burying it within their village, they can ensure that their child's attachment to their community is maintained as, despite what the future may hold, they will not wish to stray permanently from their twin. But the exact location of its burial is dictated by the child's sex and gives a telling insight into the strict sex roles that persist within this culture. Fathers will bury the placenta of their son on the nearest street corner to encourage their child to seek a future beyond the confines of the village, whereas that of their daughter will be buried as close to the family home as is practicable. A daughter's future place is with her parents. Fathers attach considerable cosmological power to the ritual of the placenta burial. Beyond its importance in anchoring a child to its ethnicity and community, it has a role in protecting the child's future well-being. Hence a man must not be distracted by his surroundings on his journey to the burial site, lest his wandering eyes lead to eye problems for his child. Likewise, the placenta must not be buried too near to water, to avoid future stomach troubles.

* * *

Becoming a father is not a moment in time, it is a process; one that can start many years before a child is born, when the desire for a child might emerge, and continue for several years after birth. But pregnancy and birth are a special time in this process of change – a time of growing recognition of a new future and a new role. This period constitutes one of life's key markers, the moment when attention shifts from the 'I' to the 'we' and life, in all its guises, is fundamentally and permanently changed.

In this chapter I want to explore dads' experiences of birth. While in many cultures birth is a time of ritual, here in the West it is more usually a time dominated by hospitals, doctors, appointments and paperwork. This has consequences for the man's experience, which, in some cases, can lead to issues coping with his new life and identity. I want to explore the causes and consequences of these issues and what the new dad can do to help his experience of birth be as positive and joyous as it can undoubtedly be.

* * *

'Couvade' is a term derived from the French word *couver*, meaning to hatch or brood, and adopted by anthropologists to describe the phenomenon present in many societies of a series of ceremonies, rituals and psychological and physiological experiences that occur as a man becomes a father. Thought to have originated in Ancient Egypt, these occurrences and experiences are deemed to be important because they help the father, kept at a distance from the physical experience of pregnancy, to adapt to his new role, assert his significance to the family and gather essential support from his community. As a consequence, they have a vital role in helping the man deal with the practical and psychological impact of becoming a parent.

Couvade is split into two distinct categories of behaviour. The first set of behaviours fall under the heading of couvade rituals and are performed by the man to involve himself more fully in the process of pregnancy and birth, to provide protection to his child and the mother or to cement his new child's place within their community. They are rituals that acknowledge both that becoming a father is a life-changing experience for a man and that the birth of a child is a community as well as individual matter. So, our Satun man will not only carry out the ritual of placental burial after birth but will fill the long pregnancy hours with practical jobs to support his wife once the baby is born, including constructing a wooden bed, the *khrae,* on which she will rest with her baby for forty-four consecutive days following birth. During this time, mum and baby will be warmed by a fire that the father will continuously tend to to ensure it doesn't go out.

Why is the couvade a significant process for the men who take part? For women, the connection to their child is physical, visceral. For a man, his connection is social – made by the interactions he enjoys with his child and the social recognition of his role. By performing couvade rituals, he is publicly taking on the mantle of the father and, more vitally perhaps, asking his community for their help and support in successfully navigating the journey from man to father. Beyond this, many rituals are also tied up with the future protection and support of the child. Picture the Thai man burying his son's placenta on the street corner. He is carrying out this ritual to ward off illness and also to encourage his child's loyalty to his community but, in addition, his choice of burial location reflects his hopes that his son's future will extend beyond the village. In these wishes are reflected two themes that I will return to again and again in this book. That is, regardless of the vagaries of time and the challenges of the environment, at the heart of every father's role is the drive to ensure his child's survival *and* to teach and guide his child so that he or she can operate separately as a successful, autonomous being when the time comes to enter the adult world.

Practices such as those of the Satun people were once widespread. But with the onset of the medicalization of childbirth, even in remote areas, the opportunity to carry out such ceremonies, particularly around birth, has diminished. For Thai men, who are traditionally excluded from birth, the moment of new fatherhood today is more likely to be marked with hospital bureaucracy and endless form-filling than the careful removal and burial of the placenta. Such ceremonies only remain for those who choose home birth or who have the confidence and time to wade through the metres of red tape that are required before a placenta can be removed from the hospital setting. But what remains in societies after these rituals have died out is an astonishing physiological phenomenon that is perhaps the body's reaction to the profound emotional and practical experience of becoming a father.

Having a kid is life-changing! It is obvious to say, but it really is ... I don't know where my time went before or what I used to do, what I spent my time doing, because I don't seem to get any time now! I mean, I have to make it, which involves getting up at stupid o'clock and doing things then.

Dylan, dad to Freddie (six months)

75

If you are a father, then Dylan's story will be familiar to you. Having a child causes an inevitable disruption to your daily routine. The demands of work and home need to be juggled, so you grab food whenever there is the opportunity and a full night's sleep is but a fond and distant memory. For many of you, these changes in lifestyle will have had a physical consequence – you put on weight. Gone are the days of frequent gym visits or Sunday morning five-a-side, to be replaced with a diet heavy in carbohydrates, fat and sugar, to fuel the long days and broken nights. But for some of you, the impact of impending fatherhood on your physical health may be more severe and striking. You might suffer stomach cramps and diarrhoea and feel listless and lacking in appetite. If this is you, then you are exhibiting the second category of couvade behaviour: couvade syndrome.

Couvade syndrome is a difficult phenomenon to grasp. Its diverse set of symptoms, which focus largely on the digestive system but can stretch to muscle cramping, loss of libido and toothache, are hard to pin down. As such, diagnosis is difficult, and men's complaints are often dismissed. One consequence of this is that we have little idea of its frequency in modern populations; global estimates from a number of studies range from 11 per cent to 50 per cent. What we do know is that it is largely a phenomenon of industrialized cultures. It is most likely to occur with first pregnancies and be at its most severe in the first and third trimester, symptoms more often than not disappear once the baby is born, and there are certain categories of father and personality types who are more likely to experience it. Teenage first-time fathers, men whose fathers were absent when they were growing up and the fathers of unplanned pregnancies are at increased risk, as are men who are closely bonded to their partner and exhibit strong empathizing skills. In addition, unluckily for them, men who are also keen to be closely involved in their partner's pregnancy increase their chance of experiencing this – in all probability, psychosomatic – syndrome.

All these men have one thing in common. They all probably experience heightened anxiety about becoming a father. For the teenage boy or son of a single mother, simple youth and inexperience or the lack of an adequate fathering role model can mean they find impending fatherhood more anxiety-inducing than most. For the father of the unplanned child, the gentle transition into fatherhood afforded by a planned pregnancy is denied him and he must quickly come to terms with this unforeseen, and possibly unwelcome, change in his circumstances. Men who are closer to their partner and more in tune with her experience may take on some of her concerns, worry and distress, resulting in this physical manifestation of a psychological state. Indeed, psychologist Anne Storey and her colleagues from Memorial University of Newfoundland, Canada, have found physiological evidence for this phenomenon. In their study of thirty-four Canadian first-time parents, fathers-to-be who experienced two or more couvade symptoms not only exhibited lower testosterone and higher prolactin levels (the hormone linked to milk production in mothers) than those who did not, making them more responsive partners and fathers, but their female partners also showed raised cortisol levels, indicating that they were experiencing significant levels of stress during pregnancy, a state of being that the men might well be mirroring.

The question remains as to why couvade syndrome exists and why it is a modern phenomenon, largely confined to developed countries. There have been numerous attempts at explanation, utilizing every argument from male envy at the female's ability to bear a child to jealousy of the foetus's close relationship with the mother. For me, the reason is more clear-cut and grounded in the father's everyday experience. It is an unconscious manifestation of the father's lack of recognition and support as he undergoes this key developmental stage. This lack of recognition and support will be particularly pertinent for those men who wish to be closely involved in their partner's experience during pregnancy or those who might require additional support due to lack of life experience or an adequate role model. Couvade rituals, as described above for our Thai father, allow men to take a distinct role during pregnancy and birth, and to display not only their new role to the community but to advertise their need for support. They find security in having a firm, socially mandated role and being clear about what it involves. Their role is acknowledged as important by their community. Within the West, where all sectors – social, commercial, medical – focus exclusively on the mother, a lack of overt couvade ritual means that fathers can struggle to identify a role and garner recognition and support for their experience. This can lead to greater anxiety and, as a consequence, the symptoms of couvade syndrome. This lack of recognition is evident in Steve's experience of antenatal care:

[The check-up] I did go to, my partner got on the seat and the midwife drew the curtain [in front of] me and my partner said, 'He can watch,' and she said, 'Oh, right,' and I thought, *Well, I am the husband … in a month's time I'm going to be seeing everything.* And the midwife was a bit weird, as though I shouldn't be there.

Steve, dad to Anna (six months)

Over the years I have spoken to many new fathers, and what is clear is that, alongside excitement, pride and fear, many men, like Steve, find the experience of pregnancy and birth marginalizes them. With the medicalization of pregnancy and childbirth, many of the processes that could have afforded an opportunity for public ritual are removed from the community to the hospital. As such, men are denied the opportunity to gain public acknowledgement of their role. Despite dad being a presence in the birthing room for nearly forty years, stories of exclusion are common. Dads who are asked to wait outside while mums are examined, questions regarding wishes for the birth or aftercare directed solely at mum, fathers left to let their worst imaginings run riot when their partner is whisked off for an emergency procedure. This exclusive focus on the mother can be to the detriment of the father's well-being – many men report being made to feel like an imposter or a spare and unwelcome part. Unfortunately, this sense of exclusion is a constant subject of discussion during my conversations with fathers:

I'm sat there thinking … *I'm exhausted helping to look after you, you've been sick all morning.* No one asks you how you are; no one ever does … Men aren't seen to be that vulnerable and that involved in the pregnancy process; the baby's not inside me, is it?

Theo, dad to Lila (six months)

What is surprising is that these experiences are from the very recent past, when it is accepted best practice, both nationally and internationally, for a father to be fully involved with pregnancy and childbirth as an equal member of the parenting team. Numerous reports from bodies as esteemed as the World Health Organization and the United Nations have repeatedly stated that fathers should be fully included in all decisions and processes surrounding pregnancy and birth for the good of the mother, the baby and the man. Indeed, a number of recent studies have reported that the health outcomes for mum and baby, and the continuing health of the new family, are improved by fathers being involved in all aspects of antenatal care and birth. But such reports don't appear to have influenced real-world practice. This sense of being a bystander is not just voiced by the men I have interviewed in the UK; it is a problem that is evident across Western culture. In her analysis of pregnancy and birth experiences from nine countries, including the UK, Sweden, the USA, Japan, South Africa and New Zealand, Mary Steen, a professor of midwifery at the University of Chester, summed up the overall experience of fathers as being that of someone occupying the no man's land between being a patient and being a visitor. They are not undergoing a physiological process that requires medical intervention, hence they are not a patient, but they are also not in the category of hospital visitor; they are more than this. They are undergoing a life-changing experience alongside their partner, which, within medical circles, defies definition. And as it defies definition, no one quite knows what to do with them, either emotionally or physically. Steen recounts an incidence where one father was asked to stand in the corner and 'not interfere' during birth, and concludes that while men are now regularly in the birthing room, they still feel excluded from the process, even though physically present. Again, the dads in my study echo this experience:

> Since getting home with our baby, the midwives would come, the health visitors would come, and even though I'm here, they don't really acknowledge me, that I'm here. I don't think there is any real support there for fathers, and if something had gone wrong at any stage, I don't think there was anyone there to support the father. When the health visitors were here, no one said to me, 'How are you?' It was almost as if I were intruding, coming into the room when Kate was talking to the health visitor. It was like, 'Huh, you're here as well? Okay.' It was like they didn't know how to deal with it. But why should I not be here? He's my son as well.
>
> *David, dad to Harry (six months)*

Why does it matter how fathers are treated by healthcare professionals? Why should we be concerned that they are having to deal unsupported with significant psychological, if not physiological, change during the period encompassing pregnancy and birth? It matters for two main reasons. Firstly, fathers who are involved in pregnancy and birth are much more likely to be involved fathers after birth. Numerous studies among all socio-economic classes and ethnicities of father have shown that by involving a father from the early stages of pregnancy you are instilling in him a habitual routine that will naturally continue after birth. This is of importance to him because fathers who have an identifiable role are much more likely to transition to parenthood smoothly, which in turn will have a positive and significant impact on his partner and child. One of the key, and arguably easiest, ways health and social care practitioners can make sure fathers feel involved and encourage them to take on a role is to *acknowledge them as a significant player*. It is a simple and cost-neutral act to ensure they are included in all discussions regarding their baby, to enquire after their health and well-being, listen to their queries and concerns and support them in their chosen role during pregnancy and at the birth. To empower them to embark on the process of becoming a dad. Those of us who research and campaign for fathers just need to find an effective way to get this message across.

The second reason for recognizing dads during pregnancy and birth is that, alongside the quality of his relationship with his partner, how well a father navigates the journey to fatherhood is significantly impacted by how he is treated by healthcare staff. The transition to fatherhood can last a significant period of time, up to two years after birth, compared to around nine months in mothers, meaning that, arguably, fathers may require support for longer than mothers. And it can include some key points of change that have the potential to cause significant distress. Many of these can occur in the first few weeks after the birth, when the resources available to dads – professional and personal – are probably at their lowest. These significant events are the birth itself, the immediate post-birth period and the return to work. For many men, the birth is a time with huge emotional and practical consequences. There is the need to cope with your own psychological and emotional experience and to identify a practical role within the birthing room. Again, in some cultures a series of couvade rituals define this period and provide a clear route for dad to follow that can ease his anxiety. In both historical and contemporary non-industrialized societies, such as the aboriginal people of Australia and the Basques of Spain, men are reported to imitate the behaviours of their pregnant partner – withdrawing from work, displaying swollen stomachs and, when the day of birth itself arrives, remaining in their bed and imitating the sounds and actions of labour. Significantly, many of these men will be excluded from the birth itself, unlike fathers in the West, but will ensure their involvement and cement their bond with their wife and child by this public display. Without such prescribed public rituals to fall back on, it is this need to identify a role during birth that often causes dads in the West the most difficulty. And being among the first generation to enter the birthing room, there are few traditions to follow or role models to emulate.

There was never a doubt I was going to be there no matter what, completely. My mum said she wanted to come down to the hospital and be there, but we said, 'No, stay away, this is our moment for us, we want it to be just us.' So, I was always going to be there, I was never going to be anywhere else. I wasn't going to pass out either! Although after she was born, I did sit down for one moment . . .

Neil, dad to Libby (six months)

Within the UK, the most recent government statistics suggest that 96 per cent of fathers will be present at the point of their child's birth. Having fathers at the birth is an overwhelmingly positive thing for them and their family; it increases the likelihood of a father being involved with his child long-term, acknowledges that having a baby is a shared experience within the couple and allows for the commencement of bonding between dad and baby at the earliest opportunity. For the dads I interviewed, being able to see their baby's first breath, to hear their first cry is a life-changing and unforgettable moment. And for many men, being there allows them to achieve some significant 'firsts' – first hold or first nappy change – enabling them to feel they have had a unique experience with their child. For one of my dads, Frank, the consequence of a rather traumatic birth that left his wife requiring some medical attention meant that through all the stress and difficulty, a silver lining emerged. He was not only the first to hold his baby but got to spend an exclusive hour with him, one on one.

There was quite a situation [after the birth], but during that time I just had him, and that was actually very special because for an hour I had a first special bonding, chatting to him . . .

Frank, dad to Tom (six months)

Frank's experience is reflective of that of most men, even those who experience the most objectively straightforward birth. It is a time of hugely contrasting emotions, a real roller coaster. The excitement of realizing labour has commenced is quickly replaced by the anxiety engendered by an unknowable, and uncontrollable, future. The desire to stay strong for your partner is contrasted by the distress of seeing a loved one in pain. The pride you feel as your partner goes through this most physical of experiences is balanced by your frustration when she will not heed advice that will make her more comfortable. And at the end, the overwhelming relief and joy of birth can be replaced by concerns regarding the health of your baby and partner, and the sudden awareness that your attention has now to be split in two.

> Because everyone kind of pictures it that it would be a case of baby is delivered, baby is given to mum, mum's on the hospital bed holding the baby, then I can come over and it is the three of us together. But Liz was on the bed quite immobile, Poppy's on the other side of the room being looked at by the doctors and there definitely was a moment where I thought, *Who do I go to?* I definitely felt, *I don't want to bother anybody, but I am worried about both of them.*
>
> *Nigel, dad to Poppy (six months)*

For fathers sitting at the centre of the whirlwind of feelings that accompany birth, not having the support of the professionals who surround you and your partner can make you feel like the most insignificant person in the room. In the terminology of Mary Steen, what fathers actually need is to be helped to identify an authentic role and then fully supported in acting out that chosen role by those around them. What this role might be is entirely open to the father and his partner. Together you may decide you will be her advocate, giving voice to her needs and desires when she might be otherwise unable to speak. Or you may take on a practical role, timing contractions, providing physical support, even using your body as a scaffold, as she labours:

> I was actively involved in the birth, which I really enjoyed; I like actually having a part and holding legs up and things, that was really good … cutting the cord. But there were other bits I had to look away from … bits I didn't feel comfortable with and [I] had to turn away, but afterwards, when you get to the end, it is completely worth it.

> *Theo, dad to Lila (six months)*

Or you and your partner may decide that you, the father, will not attend. All of these are personal choices that need to be made within the couple before birth and then supported, without judgement, by those within the birthing room and beyond.

It can be no surprise to hear that even for fathers who experience a relatively stress-free transition to fatherhood, becoming a new dad requires huge amounts of practical, emotional and intellectual resources. There is so much to learn in a short period of time, and it is often very clear that the baby has not read the manual you have. Watching your baby develop is one of the great joys of parenthood – the first time they smile, sit unaided, babble or walk – but for parents, this also means that the rate of change can be fast and you need to run to catch up. Your baby's first steps are wonderful, but then having to move all the ornaments away from baby's reach and tackle the complexities of stair gates is not so much fun. However, I would say that the overwhelming opinion of the fathers I have worked with over the years is that, with time, it becomes easier to keep up – you become better at the job of fatherhood, your baby starts to repay your dedication with the most wonderful opportunities to interact, and you get more sleep! Henry's experience is pretty typical:

Our lifestyle has changed completely, in ways for the better, but it is a massive struggle; it's like taking on another job almost, because it has been very tiring, a lot of hard work, a lot of sleepless nights . . . The further you go back, the worse it was . . . learning everything, being a dad for the first time, everything is brand new . . . I think when it started off, she was such a responsibility, she was such a . . . 'burden' is not the word . . . she was such hard work that I think it is difficult to build a bond straight away . . . I think your resentment of 'you are making me get up at this time, making me do this again' is quite overpowering, but as they get older you play with them more, see their personality . . . your bond grows.

Henry, dad to Ruby (six months)

It is truly the case that, like for Henry, becoming a father will test you to your very limits and cause you to dig deep on a quest for mental and physical resources that you didn't even know you had. But for some fathers, the period before and after the birth can be tougher than for most, as Colin explains:

> You do get a bit depressed. You do get a bit down, because your life isn't what it used to be and you kind of doubt yourself and you doubt whether you made the right decision to be a dad. You doubt whether you're going to be good at it because you think, *This is my child, I shouldn't be feeling this tired. I shouldn't be feeling this resentful.* Anxiety and doubt creep in as well, because you want to make sure you made the right choice and that you are the right kind of father.
>
> *Colin, dad to Freya (six months)*

Postnatal depression in mothers is a phenomenon with which we are all familiar, and mothers are assessed regularly both during pregnancy and for up to a year after birth to ensure that cases are caught and treated early. It can be the most debilitating condition and have a profound effect on the woman, her baby and family. But it is only very recently, in the past five years, that the possibility that fathers can also suffer from this condition has been entertained. Indeed, it is only with the move towards encouraging involved fathering and with the acknowledgement that many fathers wish to co-parent their children that the idea that becoming a father may be as profound an experience as becoming a mother has been part of the discussion. But we now know that fathers bond with their babies just as deeply and profoundly as mothers, that fathers have a unique and separate role to play in their child's development and that fathers undergo a shift in their hormone profile akin to that which occurs in mothers. All of this suggests the possibility that dad as well as mum may be vulnerable to mental ill health as a result of this key life transition. Mark's experience is not unusual:

> I had had the first week of elation – 'Look what I have done' – which was obviously great, and then I started to get, I guess, the baby blues. I thought, *Hold it, she doesn't seem to respond to me.* I felt like – it sounds weird – but I felt like I didn't get a good vibe from my baby. I didn't think I was doing anything right.

> *Mark, dad to Emily (four) and George (three)*

While the research on paternal mental health is still at an early stage, sufficient studies have now been carried out to give us some idea of the nature of this condition in men. In their summary of sixty-three global studies of postnatal depression (PND), published in 2015, Karen-Leigh Edward and her colleagues from the Australian Catholic University found that the rate of PND in fathers rested at around 10 per cent, compared to 14 per cent in mothers, and that this was significantly higher than the rate of depression in a comparable population of non-fathers of between 7 and 8 per cent. This would suggest that, rather than being a symptom of age or lifestyle, these men were suffering with poor mental health as a result of becoming fathers. But what is of more significance is the fact that the nature of PND in men differs significantly from that in women. In men, the key risk factors are whether the mother has PND – this is known as co-morbidity – and the quality of the relationship between mum and dad. Further, feeling a sense of exclusion from the mother–infant relationship, finding a significant gap between the expectation and reality of new fatherhood, balancing home and work life and financial concerns also increased the risk for fathers of suffering from this debilitating condition. Dads who have PND tend to experience more anxiety, aggression, distress and doubts about their parenting than mothers, and this can cause them to withdraw from the family and turn to forms of self-medication – generally alcohol or drugs – to ease their symptoms. In their study of parental loneliness, Niina Junttila and colleagues from Turku University in Finland found a strong relationship between the levels of emotional and social loneliness in fathers and the incidence of depression – men with PND were more likely to report a lack of social contact and support and an absence of a close bond within their relationship. Finally, the trajectory of paternal PND differs from that of mothers. While for mothers the key risk period for PND is during the first year after birth, for fathers the arrival of their child's first birthday is the critical moment when their period of risk commences, midway through their transition journey. Perhaps the accumulation of stressors over the first year of fatherhood becomes too much for some.

For fathers, acknowledging and coping with poor mental health during pregnancy and in the period following birth can be a challenge, due to prevailing attitudes in society towards masculinity and mental illness and a lack of targeted services for fathers. In her 2017 study, Zoe Darwin from the School of Healthcare at the University of Leeds interviewed nineteen fathers who had reported symptoms of poor mental health during the perinatal period – that is during pregnancy, birth and the first year after birth. She found that fathers had difficulty acknowledging their feelings – referring to their poor mental health as stress, rather than depression or anxiety – felt that they did not have a right to feel down and believed that they were not entitled to look for support from health or social care professionals. They experienced considerable guilt, as they felt they were letting their partner and baby down, and especially guilty if they were driven to access limited professional resources that they felt should, by rights, be given to their partner. Those who did want to seek help were unsure of how to because of the weak relationships they had developed with healthcare staff – their contact being limited to, at most, accompanying their partner during the all-too-brief antenatal appointments. They felt underprepared to be fathers and struggled as their previous tactics for handling workplace stress – distraction or avoidance – failed to lessen their feelings in this context. This made them feel less than 'real men', as their role of protector was replaced by the need to be protected. However, in the absence of formal support, men did identify some tactics that helped them to get over the most severe periods. Some found reminding themselves that the speed of change with a new baby, a cause of stress in its own right, was also, ironically, a positive, as most difficult phases did not last for long. Others found that carving out specific daddy and baby time helped – the opportunity to bond one-on-one allowed dad to achieve competency in his new role, and the smiles and giggles of their baby had powerful mood-lifting effects. Others found that playing sport or relying on the advice and support of their established social networks – friends, family and work colleagues – was a huge help in giving them a break from the relentless nature of some aspects of parenting and normalized their experiences. Colin was one of the dads in my study who was diagnosed with postnatal depression:

> I mean, I was signed off recently for stress, which was a new thing for me, [I'd] never been signed off before. I was off for two weeks. It was probably my fault as well, because I got a new job as she was born, so a new job, a new baby, it was fantastic. A lot of responsibility added on at work, a lot at home, so it all mingled into one. So, a lot of anxiety and depression, but it all stemmed from stress because I took on too much. And it was definitely the result of what was happening at home, because it affected work – lack of sleep, and I had so much less energy. I was taking on more work and my memory was going through the roof, I couldn't remember what I was supposed to do at work, I couldn't remember where I was supposed to be. So, that wasn't good. Just a complete nightmare for a time.
>
> *Colin, dad to Freya (six months)*

As an academic community, we are only just coming to terms with the extent of poor mental health within the population of fathers within the UK. Government and society are even further behind. As a specialist in this area, I am asked to join radio and TV discussions about the 'existence' of paternal PND on a reasonably regular basis and, while a hot topic with journalists, the normal response I see is less one of empathy and more one of 'all these men need to pull themselves together and stop moaning – they haven't given birth'. A depressingly narrow-minded response and one that, you would hope, would not be directed towards a woman in a comparable situation. Because paternal PND is real and it carries a cost. There is the obvious cost to the father, but if that does not motivate someone to listen and act, then there are the costs to the child's development, to the happiness and cohesiveness of the family and to our society, in terms of treating and policing the increased antisocial behaviour and addiction that can arise further down the line in the children of depressed parents. So, realizing that we are unlikely to get fathers the tailored support they need without appealing to the economics of the situation, several researchers have tried to put a price on poor paternal mental health.

The immediate and long-term cost of poor maternal mental health in the UK is around £6.6 billion each and every year; 60 per cent of which is related to the costs to the child of the negative impact on their development (for example, additional behavioural and educational support services or police and court costs associated with anti-social behaviour). It is likely, with the independent influence that a father has on his children's development and the particular responsibility he has for their social behaviour and long-term mental health, that the cost of poor paternal mental health is within the same ballpark. Within Australia, the cost to the system of paternal PND was $18 million in 2012 alone. In the first study of its type within the UK, a team from the universities of York, Warwick and Oxford, which included my colleague, psychiatrist Paul Ramchandani, calculated that for each and every man who presented with symptoms of PND it cost the NHS, at the most conservative estimate, an additional £158 as compared to a man without PND. This may sound like an insignificant sum compared to £6.6 billion, but if we remember that the rate within our population of paternal PND is around 10 per cent of fathers *and* that this sum does not include the use of any specific father-targeted programmes of intervention, only drugs and GP costs alone, *and* excludes the cost to the child's development and our society in terms of policing or social care, it is a considerable amount of money.

So, what can be done? At this point in time, in the absence of specific, father-focused interventions, we have to fall back on established systems of antenatal and postnatal education and try to find some space in there for dad. In their recent meta-analysis of the impact that established interventions have on the mental health of dads, Australian psychologists Holly Rominov, Pamela Pilkington, Rebecca Giallo and Thomas Whelan were able to assess which methods were the most effective for preventing paternal PND. They found that one of the most effective techniques was to train dads to deliver massages to their partners and, once born, their babies. Massage is often one of the techniques that dads are taught during antenatal classes to help them feel involved in their partner's pregnancy and, following birth, to find them an exclusive role during the first few weeks of their baby's life, when they can often feel excluded. But Holly and her team found that an added bonus was that, in repeated studies, it helped reduce depression and anxiety in fathers. With the insight we have from neuroscience, it is clear that dad, baby and partner gain a neurochemical reward from these interactions, making it a win-win all round. Touch is one of the most effective ways of releasing the feel-good chemicals oxytocin, dopamine and beta-endorphin, and this flood of positive chemicals in dad's brain counteracts the release of the stress hormone cortisol and improves his mental health. From a psychological standpoint, by learning a skill he also gains confidence in his competency as a dad, which raises his self-esteem.

The other intervention that Holly and her team identified as having a positive impact on paternal mental health was the traditional antenatal class – but with a twist. It is not unusual for dads to attend antenatal classes with their partners to learn about pregnancy, birth and baby caretaking, but in most cases they are there in a supporting role. However, there is a growing recognition that fathers benefit hugely from male-only antenatal classes. In an era of global austerity, these classes are thin on the ground, but where they do exist, even in the form of one men-only class out of the usual run of six or eight couples' classes, they have a profound impact on a man's mental health. Being able to take part in one of these classes allows men to relinquish their role as 'emotional rock' and speak freely about their fears and anxieties, focus on the skills that will help them as a dad and ask all the questions that they fear may make them look stupid in front of an audience of mums-to-be. The classes are particularly beneficial where the teacher has seen fit to invite a few experienced fathers, as it is increasingly becoming apparent that men feel most comfortable asking questions of and gathering information from their peers. And this can mean that sometimes they find support in the most unlikely of places.

The Lions Barber Collective is an international organization first established in the UK. It brings together a group of leading barbers, all of whom have an interest in tackling the worryingly high rate of male suicide and raising awareness of men's mental health. For years, those of us who wish to support men who struggle with their mental health have found it difficult to make contact and find suitable and effective interventions that encourage men to talk about their experiences. The Lions Barber Collective, all members of which are trained as mental health support workers, is effective because it exploits the often close and long-term relationship that men build with their barber and the confidentiality of barber chair chat to encourage men to open up about their lives. An added bonus is that men do not often include their barber in their social circle, so they do not feel the need to edit their stories to protect others. This scheme has garnered huge amounts of attention, and deservedly so, because it works. It acknowledges that men find it difficult to actively seek out help, that they need something they can access easily in their daily lives and that they will often speak more readily to a friend or acquaintance – barber, fellow sports team member – than a professional. While not explicitly focused on perinatal mental health in men, it is a model that we can follow to attempt to provide the much-needed support that fathers require.

Our understanding of paternal mental health is growing. As I finished writing this chapter, a new study by the University of Southern California confirmed a long-held hunch that, as with maternal PND, hormones have a part to play in paternal PND. As a dad, while the drop in testosterone that accompanies fatherhood is good for redirecting your focus onto your family, it increases your risk of suffering from PND; it has long been known that high levels of testosterone are a protective factor against depression. In this case, men in the study with the lowest levels of testosterone were the most likely to report depressive symptoms. Not good news if you are one of these men, but the greater the knowledge we have of this condition the more likely it is that we can work to prevent and cure it. The challenge for those of us within the field is to take this knowledge and make it generally known. To continue to voice the reasons, probably in the language of economics rather than empathy, for providing men with targeted support and intervention. At present, much of the research focuses on prevention rather than cure and, in the absence of professional help, there is certainly much a man can do during the lead-up to the birth, and afterwards, to help his mental health. This can include making use of all the tools modern technology has to offer in seeking your own support network:

> I am part of a Facebook group, which is fantastic because you get everything from a dad reporting in ... ('It's Jeff here, reporting from the dog house, I've done x or y') to difficult subjects like a dad trying to keep in touch with his kids following divorce. There are always dads in similar positions to you that you can relate to. It's really useful.

> *Ben, dad to Rosie (eighteen months) and one on the way*

If you are an expectant dad, the nine months of pregnancy are a wonderful opportunity to discuss with your partner your thoughts and concerns about your role during pregnancy, birth and beyond. You can take the time to discuss how you will work together as a parenting team and identify possible points of tension and how you can resolve them. You can use the time to pep up your massage skills and to build your own support network consisting of friends, family, professionals, colleagues and virtual groups. There is a growing number of online support communities just for dads, which many men, like Ben, find invaluable.

It had gone from this ridiculous thing of lasting for so long to all of a sudden you've got a baby, and everyone's going out the room, and there's all this blood everywhere and you've just seen the baby's head come out. It's 'oh my god' and there he is. And I just wanted to tell people; it was a really proud moment, I guess. Yes, it was just a really proud moment and I couldn't wait ... because there's not much you can do then, apart from hold him. I wanted to tell everyone, 'Look, I'm a proud dad.'

Zac, dad to Aidan (six months)

Some of the issues or points of tension that you encounter around birth will be personal to you, but from my own research I know that some have the potential to be universal. Many fathers can struggle finding a space to connect with their baby during those first intense months, particularly in the early stages when a baby may be with mum for long periods of breastfeeding. It is important that you explore how you will feel about this. Some fathers are content to be mum's supporter at this stage, knowing that their time will come, but others find it helps to identify an exclusive activity that will be just for them and their baby; bath time, the midnight bottle or the pre-bedtime massage are often popular. While some hospitals now offer family rooms that enable dads to stay after birth, these are still thin on the ground and many dads do find themselves out on the streets once baby has been delivered – the hospital car park at 3 in the morning can be a very bleak and unwelcoming place. For some fathers, the sharp contrast between the drama of birth, the joy of becoming a family and the swift ejection onto the street once mum is settled on the ward can be very difficult to take. If this is a likelihood, then identify someone who you can ring to talk to or meet once you leave the hospital, whatever the hour. Someone who can help you celebrate, reflect, laugh and cry, and provide you with a much-needed meal and drink. And whatever birth plan you have, you will be interacting with healthcare staff. Discuss with your partner how you both want to approach these interactions so that *both* your needs and concerns are addressed and so that you are supported in your chosen role.

* * *

One thing I wasn't prepared for is I find her really, really funny. It's got to be her reaction. Everything is amazing and new for her, and exciting. She seems to never get tired of stuff. Genuinely most times when we're interacting, at some point she will do something that just cracks me up.

Nigel, dad to Poppy (six months)

For the majority of men becoming a dad, while tough at times, is a period that is overwhelmingly characterized by joy – the happiness engendered by seeing life anew through your baby's eyes, the beaming grin and open arms that greet you when you get home from work, the shared experience of learning together. Ben is dad to 18-month-old Rosie and has one on the way. All parents-to-be could do well to remember his sage advice:

> To all the men who are friends of ours who are starting to think about becoming a dad, I am overwhelmingly positive. It is absolutely amazing, it changes your world, it makes everything lighten up, you have a reason to bounce out of bed most times. If I realize Rosie is up, then fantastic. If you weigh the positives and the negatives, the positives win outright. Yes, there is dealing with nappies and being woken up, but they always have that cheeky smile. I absolutely love being a dad.

Holly Rominov's work on baby massage and men-only antenatal classes has shown us that, even without great investment, there are small things that can be done to ease the symptoms of poor mental health; taking time out for yourself away from the family to do something you enjoy, using massage as a way to connect with your baby and partner and lighten your mood, building a support network of peers – in the real world or online – so you can share your feelings and be acknowledged and supported. And if your symptoms become overwhelming, then the therapies that are available to all those who suffer with poor mental health are also available to you. Taking the step to talk to a professional – midwife, health visitor or GP – is often the first step towards recovery.

Ultimately, prevention is better than cure and we all have a role to play in this. We may no longer have a tradition of couvade rituals in the West, but as fathers become more and more involved with their children, maybe we need to begin a new set of traditions aimed at recognizing and supporting men as they endeavour to successfully navigate this life-changing journey. At the very least, we can acknowledge that pregnancy and birth happen to dads too. If you are reading this as a way to better understand and support your partner or friend, take the time to ask how he is and listen with empathy to his response. Offer to babysit so he can take a well-earned break. Get a group of experienced and inexperienced dads together so that questions can be asked and issues discussed in a supportive atmosphere. Or go the whole hog and throw him a daddy-shower. When a baby is born or adopted, then it is generally the case that two people are commencing on the journey of parenthood and at least one of them is likely to be a dad. Let's make sure we are all there to support and celebrate with him.

CHAPTER FIVE

A Multitude of Dads

Dads, Flexibility and Child Survival

I want to introduce you to four fathers.

Ota is a member of the Aka tribe, who reside deep in the lush forests of the Democratic Republic of Congo. They are a hunter-gatherer tribe who hunt for small forest animals using nets. Net hunting is a whole-family endeavour, with children accompanying their mothers and fathers in their treks through the forest. Because the family is always together, Ota shares the care of his children equally with their mother and he is just as likely to sing to, comfort, feed or bathe them as she is. Indeed, he is more likely to share his bed with their children than his wife and he may even offer a crying baby his nipple to suckle until mum is available to breastfeed.

Next, meet Mike. Mike is a commercial lawyer from Boston in the United States. He works long hours and rarely sees his children during the working week, but he is driven to earn a high wage so that his children can benefit from a private education and live in a nice part of the city. He is a member of the local country club and at the weekends he takes his younger children to swimming club while his eldest son often joins him on the golf course with his work colleagues.

Next, there's Sigis. He is a father from the Kipsigis tribe in the highlands of Kenya. The Kipsigis are farmers whose predominant crop is tea. Sigis sees his main role as being the family breadwinner and spends little time with his younger children. However, when his sons reach late childhood, he begins to teach them about the farm so that they will be able to take over its running when they are adults. From adolescence onwards, he likes to spend the majority of his leisure time with his sons, leaving his adolescent daughters to his wife.

Finally, meet James. James lives in Somerset in south-west England. He is the primary carer of his three children. His wife, a successful PR executive, works in Bristol and often travels abroad, so he is the main source of practical care and emotional support for his kids. James is responsible for taking his two eldest children to and from school and carrying out the domestic chores. He is a dab hand at juggling the ballet, football and frequent play dates that make up his children's post-school itinerary, as well as providing tea and homework support and being an enthusiastic member of the school's Parent Teacher Association. Now that his youngest is in pre-school four mornings a week, he is trying to build up a copywriting business from home.

Four different fathers from four very different regions of the world, with four very different ways of fulfilling the fathering role. Who would you say was doing the better job?

In this chapter, I want to explore what drives the diversity of fathering around the world. I want to introduce you to the many different ways of being a dad, which hopefully will achieve two goals. Firstly, I hope to provide reassurance to those of you who might be embarking on this journey that there is no 'right way' to be an involved dad and, secondly, to show you that you may approach your role in a variety of different ways, but for all of you there is an underlying shared goal that ultimately moulds your approach: the powerful drive to ensure your children's survival. As dads, you might have your differences, but ultimately you are all members of the same club.

As a dad, you are free from the biological bounds of pregnancy, birth and breastfeeding, but it should be clear from previous chapters that the role you eventually adopt within your family is not quite as free a choice for you as it would at first appear. There is an element of your behaviour that is driven by evolutionary history and biology and a part that is shaped by the social, cultural and political milieu you inhabit. If we consider that modern dads can live in societies whose systems differ as markedly as monogamy and polygamy, whose politics can lean from the far right to the far left, whose inheritance systems could be patriarchal, matriarchal or egalitarian and whose economy can be founded on the principles of capitalism, communism, barter or self-sufficiency, it is hardly surprising that the dads of the world inhabit their role in a seemingly infinite number of ways. But if we add to this the influences of history, religion and politics, combined with individual differences in upbringing and genetics, it is no surprise that there are so many different ways for you to fulfil your role.

The flexibility that underpins a father's role is critical for human survival because, restricted by the high energetic and physical demands of pregnancy, childbirth and breastfeeding, the role of human mothers is tightly prescribed. In contrast, the role of a father can quickly respond to even the tiniest shift in the social, economic or physical environment that might threaten his family's survival. And this means that the role of a father can differ markedly not only between cultures but within families, between neighbours and even within the lifetime of one man. This has two consequences. Firstly, that while taking inspiration from other fathers – your own dad, your next-door neighbour, David Beckham – it is a good idea not to compare yourself to others to too much of an extent, as it is very likely that the factors influencing survival in your children's lives differ to those of your role models. Secondly, dads in apparently very similar environments can come up with starkly different ways of solving the survival puzzle, because the other elements in their life differ. So, in answer to the question I posed at the start of this chapter, it is not about who does it best but about the fascinating ways all dads arrive at different solutions to the same conundrum.

Recall the Aché fathers from Chapter Three? Like the Aka man above, they gain resources via the process of hunting and gathering but *unlike* the hands-on Aka man, they have very little to do with the direct care of their children. In their war-torn society, ensuring survival is as basic as protecting the very life of your family on a day-to-day basis. In contrast, the life of the Aka, deep within the rainforest, with plentiful food and few threats, is one of comparative egalitarian bliss. Aka fathers are the most hands-on dads in the world, spending on average 47 per cent of their day in physical contact with their children. So, one type of subsistence economy but two very different fathering styles. They differ because the social environment in which they live is so starkly different and, as a consequence, the actions that ensure the survival of the children in each society are very different. Without an immediate threat to life, the Aka man can spend his days on family hunting trips, co-parenting and ensuring the critical survival skills of hunting are passed on to his children – the skills of which his children will learn equally from him and his wife. In contrast, without the active physical protection of their multiple fathers, the children of the Aché would be under grave risk of not surviving into adulthood. Two dads, one shared goal, but two very different methods of achieving it.

Developmental scientist Robert LeVine of Harvard University argues that it is just this element of environmental risk that is the underlying cause of much of the global and local variability in fathering behaviour. Ultimately, all fathers are concerned with the survival and future success of their offspring. However, depending upon the environment, the features of the father's input that increase the likelihood of this survival may vary. In Robert's own words, fathers make 'adjustments, consciously or unconsciously, to adapt to aspects of the environment that threaten or facilitate attainment of their parental goals'. And as environments fluctuate and differ between societies, so fathering differs. In environments with high levels of risk, be this warfare, predation or disease, a father's key role is to ensure his child's physical survival and health: the first tier of the hierarchy. Where physical survival is less at risk, but economic poverty may be an issue, the next tier argues that, safe in the knowledge his child will survive, a father should then be concerned with ensuring his child develops the appropriate skills to ensure his economic survival during adulthood. Finally, where economic survival is relatively assured, a father should then concern himself with his child's social, intellectual and cultural development. So, LeVine argues that in societies that exist on the edge of survival, such as the hunter-gatherer or domestic farmer, both parents invest hugely in nurturing their child in the first years of their life to try to get him or her through that vulnerable period when the risk of death is high. In contrast, families in industrialized nations are aware that their input must be adapted towards a child with a future. Parents must be prepared to commit time and economic resources to their child. The cliché of the middle-class parent taking great pains to stimulate their child intellectually and socially and ensure they make the most of educational opportunities is widespread and the butt of many jokes. But behind it is a serious and survival-critical mission: to prepare the child to survive and thrive in the competitive social and economic environment in which they will mature.

So, now for the ultimate test: how can LeVine's model help us to understand the different ways dads fulfil their role? Let's take another look at Ota, Mike, Sigis and James and their very different approaches to fathering. Both Ota and Sigis live within comparatively benign physical environments; there are relatively low rates of warfare and disease. But their economic reality is considerably harsher, with Ota's family experiencing a hand-to-mouth existence, requiring daily hunting trips to provide food for the family, and Sigis being under pressure to produce sufficient tea at a competitive price for the commercial market from a farm that is in an increasingly tough physical environment. In their daily lives, both focus largely on the preoccupations of the second tier of LaVine's model, those related to ensuring their children learn the subsistence skills that will enable them to be economically secure as adults. Hence Ota's children will learn as they observe and participate in the family net hunt, whereas Sigis' sons will be the focus of his teachings in a society that is largely dominated by men.

In contrast, both Mike and James live in physically and economically secure environments. For them, the risk to their children lurks within the hugely complex social world in which they will have to operate as adults. For many people, success within this environment isn't simply linked to how hard you work but what school you went to, who you play golf with and what car you drive. The two key factors that will open doors for you are who you associate with – who you know and what circles you move in – and money. Mike may not be there for every bath time or sports day, but he knows that by earning the money to send his children to the right school and allowing his eldest son to observe his social and business interactions on the golf course, he is giving his children the best foundation from which to set out on a successful life course. All those hours at the country club will ensure they know the right people and develop the correct behaviours to be accepted into their circle. Likewise, James is not his family's main breadwinner, but he is supporting his children's academic and social learning by ferrying them to after-school clubs, being an active PTA member and braving the world of homework. For both our Western dads, their behaviour acknowledges that within their environments the greatest risk to their children lies in their inability to navigate our complex and stratified social world. Strikingly, if you ask a father what worries them in relation to their children, they do not focus on what is taken for granted but what is at risk. For Ota and Sigis, this is economic survival; for Mike and James, it is the worry that their children won't achieve their social and intellectual potential. If you are a dad, then you can test out LeVine's model for yourself. Answer these two questions: What is your main role within your family? And what would you say is the greatest risk to your children? Consider your answers.

Beyond the theory, there are a number of academic studies that support the link between the presence of a father and the survival of his children. In their contemporary study of father presence and infant mortality in the state of Georgia in the US, epidemiologists James Gaudino, Bill Jenkins and Roger Rochat used birth and death certificate records to understand the link between father involvement and survival. They compared the death rate among babies whose fathers were listed on their birth certificates – they took this as an indication of their involvement – to those whose birth certificate did not name a father. It is important to know that within this state, married mothers have the option as to whether or not to list the father while unmarried mothers must gain the written consent of the dad to do so. Regardless of the socio-economic background of the mother and the general health of the baby, babies whose fathers were not named on their birth certificate were 2.5 times more likely to die in their first year of life. That is quite some statistic. Gaudino and his team concluded that the data seemed to support the notion that fathers had a vital role to play in their children's health.

Why does it matter that we can find a link between the presence of a dad and a child's chance of survival in the data? Because the story of the evolution of fatherhood that we encountered in Chapter One relies on the absolute need for fathers to turn away from a world characterized by the drive to find ever more partners, and settle for a life of domestic and familial bliss to ensure the survival of their children and, indeed, our species. Secondly, the possibility that no link will exist between child mortality and dads investing in their children has been used to suggest that dads aren't actually all that important – an argument that you might have realized I strongly disagree with. A case in point is the 2008 study 'Who keeps children alive?' by sociologist Rebecca Sear and anthropologist Ruth Mace. They collected data from forty-five historical and contemporary populations about who carried out childcare and the rate of child mortality within that society. As our evolutionary story would predict, in all societies the data supported the idea that mum couldn't raise her children without help from at least one relative. But this person was most likely to be her mum, the children's maternal grandmother, rather than their dad. Indeed, dad only had a positive impact on child survival in one third of the societies. This rather argues against the idea that dads are essential to the survival of their children. But I'm not about to panic and rewrite Chapter One quite yet, because many of the studies Rebecca and Ruth used involved children of less than five years of age and, as will become clear, many dads in the West really step into their role during late childhood and adolescence, particularly when the time comes to teach their children. It's that all-important role in preparing children to step into the big wide world again. Rebecca and Ruth's study did not cover this period. Second, as is clear from Robert LeVine's model, ensuring physical survival is really only critical to those dads who live in environments that cause them to sit on the first tier of the parenting hierarchy. If you are a dad in the West, then your motivations and activities will be different: social and economic survival are key. And sometimes that can mean being content to operate dad's free taxi service rather than bravely protecting your children from the invading hordes.

* * *

The role of a parent is made up of countless tasks, just ask Simon.

> I'm not aiming to be an ideal dad, because I feel I need to straddle two roles. I really feel I need to be really nurturing and really available, and [also to be] teaching and setting boundaries and all that stuff. I want them both to be powerful and brave and all those things. I always say to them the most important thing to be is kind.

> *Simon, dad to Daisy (six) and Bill (five)*

111

Some tasks are very practical and immediate; preparing food, changing nappies, providing a comforting hug or being a source of entertainment. Others are a bit less hands-on; ensuring there is food on the table, a fire in the hearth and a secure home. And some will only bear fruit a long way in the future; building social networks to get that crucial work experience gig or saving money for college fees. To help define the sorts of tasks an individual dad or mum may carry out, we can make the distinction between direct and indirect parental care. So, caretaking, teaching and carrying a child are classed as direct care – care that involves you being hands-on and in close physical proximity to your child. Indirect care – such as protection, provisioning and building social alliances – occurs at a distance from your child but is, nevertheless, as vital to their survival as the more hands-on aspects of direct care. Until very recently, there was a distinct sexual division of parenting roles in the West; dads provided indirect care while mums did the direct care. But with the rise of the idea of the involved father in the 1980s, this demarcation began to blur. The ideal father was now one who did both – direct and indirect. He not only had to provide the food for the table, but prepare it, feed it to his child and wash the resultant debris off said child in the bath. As we will see, fathers providing direct care is a wonderful and overwhelmingly positive state of being for all members of the family and our society, *but* it has lured fathers into the trap, already experienced by women, of not only believing they can have it all but that indirect care – being an 'old-fashioned dad' – is somehow a lesser form of parenting. This can mean that for those dads where economic necessity dictates that their balance between work and home life is skewed strongly towards work, the reality of their fathering experience may be a sense of failure and guilt that they are not doing a 'proper' job.

> [I want to be] protector, teacher, carer, all of that really. Just make sure he is safe and, well, happy and enjoying things. Showing him the world. Even before he was born, I was looking forward to teaching him things, showing him things and just being there for him.
>
> *David, dad to Harry (six months)*

When I talk to expectant fathers about what role they would like to adopt following the birth of their child, the vast majority will wish, like David, to be a co-parent. To be equally as responsible as their partner for, and adept at, the direct care of their child. They want to be equal caretakers, nurturers, comforters and teachers. Following birth this is still their hope, but for many it is a difficult goal to reach – they have not bet on the vagaries of biology, society and politics. Unless we make a dramatic advance in fertility technology, it is the case that men cannot give birth. Nor can they breastfeed. So, regardless of the wishes of the parents, for all but a very few exceptions it is the mother who will be the primary carer of the child for the initial weeks of its life. This means that not only will she provide the majority of direct care, but that she is incapable of providing the key form of indirect care – money. Meaning that dad is gener-ally the one who has to head back to work soon after baby is born. Despite political parties falling over each other to promote their family-friendly policies and everyone from TV celebrities to actors to sportsmen being drafted in to promote the idea that real men care for their children, the statistics tell a different story. Within the UK, in the period 2011 to 2012 only 0.6 per cent of new fathers made use of Additional Paternity Leave to share their wife's maternity leave and, while doubling in the decade since 1993, today only 229,000 British fathers are stay-at-home carers compared to 2.05 million women. Within the US, census data shows that in the year 2014, 2 million men were stay-at-home parents, which is twice as many as were reported in the 1989 census and a considerably higher number than the six – yes, that's six men in an entire country – who defined themselves as stay-at-home dads in the 1970 census.

My work with dads suggests that these woefully low take-up rates are not a sign of a lack of intent on dads' part to be involved but a consequence of the impossibility of success-fully navigating two hurdles that stand in the way of fathers: government policies rendered unworkable by a lack of finan-cial backing and the still-clear pay gap between men and women, which means that, financially, many couples cannot afford for dad to stay at home and mum return to work.

Men can now share paternity leave, I think it's three months off, but it's only at statutory maternity pay so it's rubbish pay anyway. You're not really encouraged to do it if you're going to get such low pay. I mean, a lot of men are the bread-winners, so why would they want to take such low money when women get so many months off at half pay or full pay, depending on the company? I think the government pay lip service to it but aren't really bothered. I would have been really interested in doing it but not for that money, not when times are this tough.

Colin, dad to Freya (six months)

Today's dad may want to be involved, but he hasn't relinquished his instinct to protect and provide, which means that taking a damaging financial risk to stay at home is, for dad, a risk to survival too far. On top of this, many men come up against an apparently immovable workplace culture that dictates that women have maternity leave and men, at the very most, take a couple of weeks of paternity leave and return to a working environment that has most likely been largely unaffected by their newly minted father status. Despite the term 'family friendly' implying that policies that allow for the accommodation of parenting within the working career should apply equally to men and women, for many men, broaching the subject of flexible working or shared parenting leave is still a daunting, uphill struggle. This means that for men like Dylan, their aspirations to be present quickly come up against the very hard reality of a deep-seated cultural antipathy towards hands-on dads:

Last week we were away on holiday for a week and I got to spend a load of time with Freddie and my wife, and it is amazing to see him grow in that space of time and how he changes. That was really great, but the problem – and this is the hard bit – is I work in London. I'm leaving the house at 6.30 in the morning before he is even awake and I get home

115

at 7.15 at night when his bedtime is 7.30. So, I'm getting fifteen minutes a day with him. Being away with him has made me realize what I am missing, and it is hard because you want to see everything, but I've still got to pay the bills. So, reality kicks in … You want to do one thing but need to do the other.

Dylan, dad to Freddie (six months)

As a result, one of the key issues for Western fathers is juggling the twin demands of wanting to provide direct care but *needing* to provide indirect care. They have hit upon the dilemma that is all too familiar to the working mother: how do you balance work and home life sufficiently well to make sure you are at least doing a pretty decent job of both? For many men, the tension that can exist between their direct and indirect roles can come as a very unwelcome dose of reality very early on in their fatherhood journey. Rights to paternity leave vary widely around the world. One of the starkest representations of the gulf that still exists between maternity and paternity rights is the fact that only ninety-two of the world's 196 countries have statutory paternity leave and in a half of these this is limited to three weeks or less. This is in contrast to the global right to maternity leave. It is hard not to view these statistics as evidence of society's continuing belief that dads just aren't that relevant in the childcare story.

Where paternity leave does exist and is adequately funded, it is overwhelmingly taken up by fathers. In the UK, where there is a statutory right to two weeks of leave, over 90 per cent of new fathers take some form of paternity leave, and my experience of interviewing dads is that it is not only a precious opportunity to come to terms with their new status and get to know the new member of the family but vital to keeping the family show on the road. Caring for a newborn is an exhausting mix of changing, feeding and cuddling and, if mum is breastfeeding, being stuck on the sofa every two to three hours with a baby that can take up to an hour to feed. As a consequence, dads are vital. They can lighten the load by being chief nappy-changer, cuddler, tea-maker and visitor-wrangler. And where mum has had a tough time at birth, they may even become their baby's primary carer as she recovers. But because of this intense involvement during paternity leave, returning to work can be a severe and unwelcome shock. Take Reuben's experience:

> I wasn't looking forward to [the return to work]. I could have stayed off for longer. I kind of dreaded coming back because it is such a stark change being at home all the time to being at work five days a week. I didn't enjoy it, to be honest. But what it has made me determined to do is work more flexibly. It changed my outlook on work. It is not going to get in the way of seeing [my son] as much as possible.

> *Reuben, dad to Charlie (twenty months)*

Dads go from complete submersion in baby world back to a workplace where it is likely their daily routine will be largely unchanged by the profound events in their home life. Indeed, it is one of the points of tension that I believe should be high-lighted to dads before their first birth, so that they can prepare emotionally and practically for this swift reality check and, if it is possible, ease this abrupt transition by using some holiday to enable a more staged return to work over several weeks. Unfortunately, the multitasking, hands-on celebrity dad is the exception, an exception cushioned by a considerable amount of money and, in all likelihood, unseen help. The question arises as to what the more regular dad battling with the twin demands of home and work – direct and indirect care – is supposed to do in these circumstances.

> Sometimes, as much as I want to help and stuff, it's not something I can really help with. Like the night-time feedings and when [my daughter] is crying and wants settling, it is Mummy that she wants. I don't know whether I feel angrier and less useful . . . it can get a bit frustrating sometimes, but it is to be expected. I definitely hope in the future, if something bad happens or she needs someone to talk to, it won't instantly be only Mum she can talk to. Kids have different relationships with their mum and their dad, I'm sure there is some scope for them both to be good relationships.

> *Nigel, dad to Poppy (six months)*

For some dads, the gap between what they had expected fatherhood to be like – true co-parenting – and the reality is less of a negative than we might envisage. For them, slipping back into the more traditional roles of maternal caregiver and paternal provider feels comfortable and allows ample opportunities to bond by being 'fun dad'. But for others, like Nigel, it can mean coming to terms with having to swiftly rethink their chosen fathering identity, having spent the nine months of pregnancy carefully honing it. If this is you, then the realization that you might not be able to be the equal parent that you wanted to be can lead to emotional upheaval. You might feel resentful that your partner gets to see the best bits of your baby during the day – the singing classes, soft play and toddler groups – while you get the grizzly, pre-bed version. Or you may feel guilty that your partner is left alone all day to deal with the challenges of a newborn while you still get your hour of uninterrupted lunch break and the welcome opportunity to stare mindlessly into space that it affords. For many of the dads I have studied, who come from all socio-economic backgrounds, the realization of the reality of twenty-first-century Western fatherhood results in change. And in a world of many competing demands on their time and attention, the thing that gives in many cases is work. In real terms, this can mean taking the risk of a financial and career hit – the less demanding job, more flexible hours, lack of promotion – to make sure you are present to teach and nurture your child:

> My job doesn't pay very well at all, it pays rubbish, but it allows me to be the father that I want [to be], because I know that if I have to go to work at six in the morning I will be back by three, and I can pick [my daughter] up from school. My plan has always been to be there for dinner and I always want to be there to help with homework in the evenings. They are the standards I have set for myself.

> *Mark, dad to Emily (four) and George (three)*

119

As we will see in Chapter Ten, where we will look at dad's influence on child development, in the physically benign but socially and intellectually challenging environment of the West, sacrificing your career to some extent has huge benefits for your child's physical and emotional well-being. But some dads go further. Where money and culture allow, the shift in priorities that becoming a dad brings can lead them to be the first to exploit the opportunity to truly turn words into action and take on the mantle of that most twenty-first century of dad roles – the stay-at-home dad:

> In March this year, Dawn went back to work and I was still setting up my business, and we needed one income coming in. So, the sensible thing was for me to look after Rosie full-time. From March until July I was the primary carer, which was fantastic. I loved it. I used to go to all the baby classes, go out with the mums and have picnics in the park. Generally, they were absolutely lovely. I think Dawn got a bit jealous sometimes when I would go off to the park with her friends!
>
> *Ben, dad to Rosie (eighteen months) and one on the way*

* * *

Why should this gap between what you imagine fatherhood to be like and the reality matter? It matters because one of the key causes of poor mental health in new dads is precisely this gap between hope and reality. Combine this with the stress caused by trying to balance work and home life, coupled, in some cases, with the pressure of being the only wage-earner in a financially strapped household, and a new dad can find himself under significant, and possibly health-breaking, strain. And, as poor mental health affects not just the man, but his partner, his child and, ultimately, society, it is a gap with which we should all be concerned. As we will also see in Chapter Ten, children need their fathers to be as present as possible to help create a healthy developmental environment. While an absent wage-earning father can pro-vide many indirect benefits that will ease a child's life course, nothing can replace the impact that spending time – however brief – with your child has on your child's psychological and behavioural development. The resolution to this tension is unlikely to be swift or straightforward; whether women can have it all is still an ongoing debate, decades on from the advent of feminism. But we do know that in those countries where the balance between work and home life is the most successful, it is often as a result of a combination of factors: carrot and stick from government, a well-funded policy and, most crucially, the voices of dads and mums clamouring for change.

It should be clear by now how incredibly flexible dads can be, ready to respond rapidly to changes in their child's cir-cumstances, all with the aim of ensuring their survival. But such behavioural flexibility cannot occur without a parallel change in the computer that drives it all: the brain. And luck-ily the paternal brain has proved itself to be just as flexible in responding to new experience as its owner. We have known for some time that becoming a mother leads to structural changes in the mother's brain; areas that enhance her maternal skills see an increase in grey matter. But it is only very recently that a similar phenomenon has been recognized in new fathers.

In 2014, developmental neuroscientist Pilyoung Kim, from the University of Denver, Colorado, recruited a group of sixteen biological dads and subjected them to MRI scans at two to four weeks following their child's birth and again at twelve to sixteen weeks to explore whether new fatherhood led to any changes in brain structure. She wanted to know whether becoming a dad had any impact on the volumes of grey matter – the actual neurons or brain cells that generate the signals – and white matter – the axons or fibres that link the neurons – in the brain. What she found was that the areas at the centre of the brain involved in attachment, the expression of nurturing behaviour and the ability to interpret and react to infant behaviour, showed significant increase in size. Interestingly, it is these areas of the brain that not only show activation during father–infant interaction but carry one of the highest densities of oxytocin receptors, suggesting that an increase in size and activation is paralleled by an increase in neurochemical reward for the father as he forms his attachment to his child. Increases in grey matter volume were also seen in the outer layer of the brain, known as the neocortex. It is here that our higher cognitive functions sit and one area, the prefrontal cortex, plays a key role in complex decision-making – something that is essential for parenting a human child. Kim's study shows us that as well as shifts in their hormone levels around the time of a child's birth, human fathers exhibit a shift in their neural structure, in response to their new role and environmental conditions, akin to that seen in mothers.

Kim's 2014 study was groundbreaking in showing us that fathers undergo just as significant an anatomical change as mums as they embark on the path of new parenthood. But in one of the most exciting fatherhood studies of recent years, Eyal Abraham, a neuroscientist from Bar-Ilan University in Israel, has built on Kim's work by studying primary caretaking fathers – in this case, his participants were gay fathers – and revealing the neural flexibility that underpins their behaviour. Generally, in the more traditional parenting team where roles are split along gender lines, we see differences between mum and dad in the areas of the brain that are activated when interacting with their child; largely the pattern is emotional centres for mum and cognitive areas for dad. This difference underpins the difference in their roles within the family, and we'll take a more in-depth look at this in Chapter Eight. But in his study, Abraham showed that the brains of primary caretaking gay dads saw activation in *both* areas of the brain and that a new neural pathway had developed to enable the two distinct areas – one at the very centre of the brain, the other on the surface – to communicate and synchronize behaviours. In this case, the flexibility of the human brain has been exploited to enable gay dads to fulfil both the mother's *and* father's roles, ensuring that the child still gets exposure to the ideal developmental environment. Whether the same is true for heterosexual primary caretaking fathers, where a mum may still be present to fulfil her role, is unclear, but what is astonishing about Abraham's and Kim's work is that they show us that dads are not only primed to instigate a swift behavioural response to environmental change but that evolution has seen fit for this fast response to be underpinned at the anatomical and physiological level as well.

If you are a dad, then you may be grappling with identifying what role to adopt in your child's life, particularly in this period of rapid change in our perception of who a dad should be. However, what is almost definitely the case is that you are approaching fatherhood very differently to the dads of only fifty years ago. And here we see our own example of the flexibility of fathering here in the West. In the space of only one generation, dads in the West have changed beyond all recognition. You are in the birthing room, sharing night feeds, changing nappies, giving baths, puréeing food and singing songs. What has changed in your environment to precipitate such a rapid turnaround in style? The causes are threefold. Firstly, you now live in a globalized world and it is less likely that you live within easy reach of your parents, meaning that you have had to step into the caretaking role most often adopted by your extended family in past times. Secondly, childbirth has become highly medicalized and incredibly swift. Instead of a nice stay in hospital, you and your partner will find yourselves processing this amazing change in your lives while trying to recall that antenatal class where you practised changing a nappy on a plastic doll, a poor substitute for the wriggling, crying infant in front of you. And thirdly, we now understand how important it is to a child's development to have their dad's input, meaning that men are feeling empowered, albeit by a society that is a bit slow to respond, to be more hands-on with their children than ever before.

The environment of fathering in the West has changed drastically and fathers, exploiting that wonderful flexibility, have changed their behaviour to meet the challenge and continue to ensure their children's survival and success. As we will see in Chapter Nine and Chapter Ten, this has had only positive consequences for children, as dads are more on hand to give their unique input and care. But while dads may share the same overarching goal, how each of you approaches fathering is a complex web of genetic and environmental factors that are unique to you. And that is the story of the next chapter.

CHAPTER SIX

Who's the Daddy?

Genes, Psychology and Hormones

Okay, let's complicate matters a little, just for fun. We now know that human fatherhood evolved as a consequence of a very real threat to the survival of our species that saw us teetering on the brink of extinction. We know that a new father experiences changes in his hormone levels and brain structure just as significant as those of his partner, which help him fulfil his role within the parenting team. We know that the role of the father is hugely flexible, enabling him to ensure the survival of his child within the fast-changing, big, wide world. We know that being a dad is about more than mere genetics; action is key. We know that the type of father a man becomes is not a free choice, but is influenced by a complex of factors including the social, ecological, economic and biological environments in which he exists, resulting in astonishing diversity. We know all this. But what is missing from this list of broad but important conclusions is the man himself. If we zoom in from the global to the individual, part of who a father is is driven by his innate biology, physiology and psychology – the elements that make him different to everyone else. In this chapter, I want to try to understand what it is about *your* unique biology and *your* unique life experience that help shape you as a dad. And to start, let's reacquaint ourselves with that most male of hormones – testosterone.

Testosterone is the hormone that gives men their broad chests, deep voices, strong jaws and famous inability to multi-task. It is also the hormone that motivates all men to find a mate and reproduce. But, as we know from Chapter Two, it is not your friend if you want to curb a wandering eye and settle down to a life of domestic bliss. We also know that to try to achieve some balance between the drive to mate and the drive to parent, which is vital to our species' survival, new fathers experience a drop in testosterone levels following birth that is hypothesized to increase their focus on the family and decrease their desire to experience the world outside the front door. But beyond this global effect, it also operates after birth at the individual level to influence the extent to which a man is motivated to be a sensitive father. And it is testosterone's role in individual differences between dads that I want to explore here.

All men have a baseline level of testosterone, and this varies between individuals. It is the reason some men are more reproductively successful than others *and* the reason some men appear to be more cut out for fathering. In one of the very first studies focusing on the neurobiology of fathering, in 2002 Alison Fleming from Emory University, Atlanta, Georgia, studied the influence of baseline levels of testosterone on the responsiveness of fathers and non-fathers to the cry of a distressed, unrelated infant (don't worry, it was a recording, no babies were prodded during the course of the experiments). Dads' responsiveness was measured via a questionnaire that asked them to rate their response on a ten-point scale with respect to ten different emotions – including annoyed, distressed, sympathetic and alert – and by measuring their heart rate. She and her team found that, firstly, fathers were more sympathetic and felt a greater urge to respond to the cry than either non-fathers or fathers who had been played a control sound – a random, unrelated sound that made sure that any results were not just the result of hearing a noise. Secondly, and more significantly for understanding variation in individual fathering behaviour, men with lower testosterone, be they fathers or non-fathers, were more sympathetic and motivated to act to help the child than those with higher levels. Fleming concluded that while testosterone does seem to influence the shift from mating to parenting, this may be partly a shift *towards* an increase in the empathetic behaviour vital to good parenting rather than simply a shift *away* from a desire to reproduce. And the differences in individual testosterone levels meant that some men found it easier and more natural to display empathetic behaviour and help the baby than others.

* * *

The human brain is a wonderfully complex organ. As we know, it is six times as large as it should be for our body size, it is dominated by a vast, many-folded neocortex that allows us to speak, learn, cheat and think, and it is capable of dictating our behaviours and desires in a range of domains – sensory, motor, emotional and cognitive – at both the conscious and unconscious level. To achieve this, it produces and is controlled by a vast array of neurotransmitters, some of which we have already encountered, which in conjunction with their receptors stimulate behaviours, prompt our senses, shape our memories, develop our thoughts and motivate us to act. It is a mesmerizingly confusing and beautiful organ to study, but among the complexity we can be sure of two things. Firstly, that it is rarely the case that one neurotransmitter acts alone and, secondly, that evolution has ensured that we carry out survival-critical behaviours by rewarding our actions with a flood of addictive, feel-good chemicals in the brain. Evolution bribes us to do the right thing. Along with the euphoria-inducing endorphins that we will encounter in the next chapter, the most studied and well-known of these chemicals is dopamine. We have met dopamine before, along with its frequent partner oxytocin, in Chapter Two, when we explored how a dad can bond to his unborn child, but it is equally as critical to your relationship with your child, and how you father, after birth. Remember, it is your go-to chemical for pleasurable feelings. It is released when we fall in love, when we drink alcohol and when we eat our favourite sugary food. And if you are a father, it is also released when you see a child.

Ten years after Fleming's pioneering research on the role of testosterone in fathering behaviour, Jennifer Mascaro, Patrick Hackett and James Rilling, anthropologists and neuroscientists, again from Emory University, used our now greater knowledge of the interconnectedness of the brain's neurochemical system and the latest advances in scanning techniques to study the interplay between dopamine, oxytocin and testosterone and their impact on individual differences in fathering behaviours. They recruited eighty-eight hetero-sexual, biological fathers and fifty non-fathers and asked them to give blood samples so that their baseline levels of testosterone and oxytocin could be measured. Following this, each man was placed in a functional MRI (fMRI) scanner – enabling their brain activity to be viewed in real time – and shown pictures of the faces of adults and children with a range of emotional expressions – sad, happy and neutral. Their results indicated some striking differences between fathers and non-fathers, and between individual dads, when viewing images of children's faces (interestingly there was no discernible difference when viewing adults). Firstly, the blood samples revealed that fathers had significantly lower levels of baseline testosterone but higher levels of baseline oxytocin – on average a third more – than non-fathers, implying that all the fathers had been hormonally primed to provide child-focused, affectionate care. Low testosterone primed their empathetic skills and high oxytocin encour-aged them to bond. Further, we know that low testosterone renders the positive effects of oxytocin on a man's fathering behaviour even more powerful, making this combination of neurochemical dosages the perfect cocktail to motivate child-to-dad bonding. Secondly, the fMRI scans showed that the areas of the brain linked to empathizing, the recognition of facial emotion and the all-important dopamine reward centres were significantly more active in dads as compared to non-fathers. So, dads were more skilled at, and focused on, reading the emotions of the children and, in return, they received a powerful dopamine reward. But within the group of dads, those who had the lowest testosterone showed the *greatest activity* in areas linked to the processing of emotional faces and the reward centres, meaning that these fathers were the *most* skilled at understanding emotion *and* received the biggest dopamine hit of all. Having low testosterone not only makes you the most focused on your family, but it also makes you more empathetic, increases the wonderful effects of oxytocin on the relationship between you and your baby and makes sure you get the biggest possible dopamine reward. It is often the case that when I tell fathers that having a child will supress their testosterone they laugh knowingly – here lies the road to emasculation. But really, trading a bit of testosterone for the wonder of your relationship with your child and one of the greatest neurochemical rewards the brain can supply isn't that big a loss, is it?

So, contrary to the long-held belief that fatherhood is a learnt rather than biological phenomenon, the increasing evidence for the role of hormones in shaping men for fatherhood makes it clear that it is a truly biological business on a par with motherhood. From the synchronizing of oxytocin levels with your pregnant partner, to the drop in your testosterone levels following birth, to the interplay between oxytocin, dopamine and testosterone, evolution has made it its business to ensure that dads are biological beasts motivated to care, protect and provide. But while our knowledge of the neurochemistry of fatherhood is growing on an almost daily basis, the complexity of the genes that underlie a man's unique cocktail of these vital chemicals, and the impact that his environment may have on their expression, is still largely shrouded in mystery.

The debate as to how much of our individual behaviour is predetermined by our genes and how much is a result of experience has raged since Charles Darwin first laid eyes on a Galapagos finch and came up with the idea of evolution and Gregor Mendel answered his green-fingered calling and produced some lovely, colourful pea plants that seemed to be a mix of their parents. In the seventeenth century, English philosopher John Locke believed we were born a blank slate – a *tabula rasa* – and that our thoughts and behaviours were shaped purely by our experience, while those who believe in genetic determinism consider us to be on a journey dictated purely by our genes and that our life experience plays no part in determining our final destination. As is so often the case, the truth lies somewhere between these two extremes. As we develop better and better techniques for analysing the genetic code and learn more about the behaviours that are influenced by our genes, we are starting to understand a few key principles about the genetic influence on behaviour. Firstly, some genes have more of an influence on our behaviour than others. Between 40 per cent and 80 per cent of antisocial behaviour is genetically determined, while a 2015 study led by geneticist Brendan Zietsch argues that the risk of being unfaithful is 40 per cent down to your genes if you are a woman and 63 per cent if you are a man – a slightly scary thought. Secondly, some behaviours are influenced by more than one gene or more than one change on a single gene. In some cases, this leads to a 'dose response', where the greater number of 'risk' genes you carry – some genes have these and they are associated with negative behaviours – the more risk there is of the negative behaviour developing or the more extreme it becomes. Finally, there is the idea that in some cases nature and nurture exist within a feedback mechanism, where a risk gene will only result in a negative behaviour *if* a certain psychological state or life experience is present. So, carrying the risk gene alone will not cause the behaviour to occur – it will only be expressed *if* particular environmental conditions are present as well.

The field of paternal genetics is very young. When we consider that fatherhood has really only been a focus for academic study for just over a decade, it is unsurprising that we have only just started to try to understand its genetic underpinnings – we have to have a solid understanding of behaviour and neurochemistry before we can start to unravel any genetic control of them. But one of the few studies that has been carried out reflects perfectly this intimate relationship between genetics and environment. In his analysis of the risk of serious and violent delinquency in African American teenage girls, sociologist Matt DeLisi, from Iowa State University in the US, studied the interaction between the dopamine receptor gene (DRD2), the presence of a criminal father and rates of recorded delinquency and police contact among the girls. DRD2 exists in a risk and non-risk form. Presence of the risk version is linked to a range of antisocial behaviours and addictions, including alcoholism and heroin dependency. In this case, DeLisi took DNA samples from the 232 girls and looked at the relationship between the presence of the risk version of the DRD2 gene and the likelihood that a girl would exhibit delinquent behaviour. What he found was that carrying this gene alone did not predict the likelihood of the girl exhibiting such behaviour – so, no evidence for genetic determinism here. But, if he also included in the analysis whether or not the biological father had a criminal record, *then* a pattern became clear. If the girl had a criminal father *and* she carried the risk version of the DRD2 gene, then she was significantly more likely to have had contact with the police due to violent and serious delinquency. The risk version of the gene was only making its presence felt in the girl's behaviour *if* dad had a criminal record. The perfect example of the co-dependency that exists between nature and nurture.

Similarly, children who carry the risk version of the dopamine transporter gene, DAT1, are only at increased risk of developing alcoholism *if* their biological father is, or has been, an alcoholic. Criminologist Jamie Vaske found, again, that when considering their impact independently neither the risk version of DAT1 nor having an alcoholic father increases their risk – the combination was key. However, in this case it did not seem to matter whether dad lived with their child or not, the impact of their alcoholism on those unfortunate enough to carry risky genes was the same. This would suggest that in this case the influence of the alcoholic father was not down to his impact on the child's environment of development but was a result of genetic inheritance – remember, dad was the biological father. A gene or set of genes that the child had inherited from the alcoholic dad, when combined with the risky DAT1 gene, led to an increased chance of alcoholism – a genetic dose response. As alcoholism is thought to be highly heritable – genetics are believed to lie behind 40 to 60 per cent of cases – the interaction of several genetic factors to cause this outcome comes as no surprise.

If we were to rely solely on the results of DeLisi and Vaske's studies, we might conclude that all children inherit from their fathers are addictions and antisocial behaviours, but this is, thankfully, very unlikely to be the case. As the field of paternal genetics is young, studies that seek solutions to society's problems are always going to get funded before those that seek to assess to what extent cuddling, coaching football or the ability to do a passable impression of a Teletubby is genetic. As time passes and the field grows, attention will shift to these more positive, and widespread, behaviours and we will start to discover all the wonderful traits that children inevitably inherit from their dads.

While individual fathering behaviour is strongly influenced by the triple cocktail of oxytocin, testosterone and dopamine, a flood of these alone is not sufficient to produce a sensitive parent – we need to ensure that the other piece of the neural jigsaw is also present: the receptor. Brain receptors are like the locks into which the neurotransmitter key fits to enable its message to be transmitted around the brain. The nature of receptors can vary between individuals in both the number within an area and their affinity for the neurotransmitter – that is, how well the lock and key fit together and how efficiently the message is conveyed. The oxytocin receptor gene (OXTR) is highly variable, meaning that it comes in many different versions and, as such, is likely to be the cause of this variability in receptor density and efficiency. The OXTR gene has been implicated in a range of behaviours linked to our social experience. These include how adept we are at using affectionate language towards our lover, how likely we are to want to form a romantic relationship in the first place, how many friends we have and how much we enjoy being sociable. It has also been implicated in the quality of fathering behaviour. Alongside it sits another nattily named gene, CD38, which has a role in the production of oxytocin and also seems to influence how a father behaves when he is interacting with his baby.

Both OXTR and CD38 have risk versions – remember this means they are linked to negative behaviours. These versions appear to be associated with deficits in social behaviour and the lower baseline levels of oxytocin that can make it difficult for the individual who carries them to form and maintain social relationships. Individuals who exhibit conditions that make it difficult for them to cope in social situations, such as autism, tend to carry risk versions of OXTR and CD38, and dads who carry them also seem to struggle with forming healthy and sensitive bonds with their children. Ruth Feldman and her team observed these difficulties in their study exploring the influence of the risk versions of CD38 and OXTR on fathers. Of the 121 fathers she studied, those who carried either one or both risk genes were less sensitive when interacting with their 6-month-old babies. When their interactions were observed, the team saw that these fathers were much less likely to touch their child affectionately and actively tried to avoid their baby's gaze, meaning that the all-important bio-behavioural synchrony that kick-starts the parent-to-infant bond was lacking. Analysis of the father's blood samples gave some idea why. Fathers who carried risk versions of the OXTR and CD38 genes had much lower levels of oxytocin – and, by association, dopamine – meaning that interacting with their baby was not the source of warm and rewarding feelings that it should have been. The neurochemical prompt to bond was just not there.

* * *

I mean, seeing my parents, they are both quite different, but seeing the friendship that I have with my parents, that is something I would like to have with Joseph. I expect him to say [frustrated], 'Oh, dad,' but, underlying that, I want to have the bigger kid sort of friendship relationship as well.

John, dad to Joseph (six months)

While genes quite clearly have a role to play in how we parent, one profound influence on our individual parenting styles is undoubtedly linked to our own experience of being parented. Early evidence of this came from a study that should win the authors a 'most dedicated scientists of the century' award. Over a period of twenty-eight years, developmental scientists Nikki Kovan, Alissa Chung and Alan Sroufe followed sixty-one families to try to understand to what extent the children of the families would mirror the parenting behaviours of their parents when they had children of their own. This meant videotaping interactions between parents and children when the children were two years old, then, having filled the intervening years with other academic activities such as drinking coffee and thinking, returning when the children had themselves become parents and their offspring were themselves two years old. Comparison of the two sets of videotapes suggested that there was a surprising degree of similarity between the parenting behaviours of the two sets of parents, as much as 43 per cent. This suggests that a significant fraction of our individual parenting behaviours is indeed inherited from our parents, but the question remains as to the exact nature of this inheritance – is it behavioural as a result of experience or genetic?

Daniel Pérusse of Montreal University in Canada set out to try to untangle this tricky web using the genetic similarity between identical twins to help him. Twin studies are a godsend to science because they rely on the fact that siblings experience identical environments as they grow up but that identical twins carry identical sets of genes, whereas non-identical twins are as genetically related as any sibling pair. If a behaviour is genetically inherited, then we should see more mirroring of behaviour between identical twins than non-identical twins, as the identical twins have more genes in common. These studies allow us to infer a role for genes without going to the huge expense of having to extract and analyse everyone's DNA, and this means we can study many more people, making our results more robust. Daniel studied the self-reported parenting behaviour of 1,117 twin pairs, all of whom had children. Of these, 675 pairs were identical; 169 male twin pairs and 506 female twin pairs. When comparing the parenting behaviours of the identical twins with the non-identical twins, he found that identical twins shared many more parenting behaviours in common, implying some genetic transmission of this behaviour. However, this similarity was stronger in female twin pairs, that is, mothers, than male twin pairs, that's the dads. Daniel calculated that, based on his results, 19 per cent of fathering behaviours were under genetic control compared to 39 per cent in mothers.

Nineteen per cent is a considerable amount of genetic control, and even more impressive when you consider how complex and extensive parenting behaviours can be – that is a lot of genes. It is amazing to think that nearly one fifth of fathering is biologically innate – that it is programmed into your genes. However, that leaves 81 per cent of the variation between individuals in fathering behaviour down to some other factor, and the number-one candidate is, inevitably, the environment – and not just any environment, but the environment in which you grew up.

We know that the development of the oxytocin pathways in the brain of a young mammal are influenced by their experience of being parented. Infants that receive optimal maternal care have higher densities of oxytocin receptors in the areas of the brain linked to social behaviour, are better able to deal with stress and are better, more sensitive parents when they themselves have a family. It is likely that the same is true with us. It takes some time for our big brains to grow and a human baby's brain continues to grow at a startlingly rapid rate for a year after birth. As such, the experiences that a human baby has of being parented during this period can have a profound effect on brain structure – hence the belief that the first 1,000 days of a child's life, that's conception to two years, are the most fundamental to their healthy development. If a child receives sensitive parenting from mum and dad during this period – a style that is nurturing but not intrusive, protective but not controlling – then he or she should develop a healthy brain and a strong and secure attachment both now and in any future relationships.

One way to achieve this goal is to encourage synchronous

behaviours between baby and parent – to mirror each other through body language, speech, sound and emotion. This means sharing gaze, mirroring body language, responding to invitations to speak or play and being alive to baby's emotions and needs. If a parent can achieve this, then the bio-behavioural mechanism will kick in – remember this is the mechanism by which parents achieve synchrony in oxytocin levels during pregnancy, leading to a strengthened bond. Likewise, baby and dad will achieve emotional, physiological and hormonal synchrony and, ultimately, a strong and healthy attachment between baby and parent will develop. It goes without saying that the originator of this hypothesis, Ruth Feldman, has tested it. In her long-term study of sixty Israeli families, she has shown that there *is* a significant positive relationship between a child's baseline oxytocin level when they are three years old and that of his or her parents. This suggests that the synchrony in behaviour and physiology – heart rate, blood pressure and body temperature – *does* result in a synchrony in hormone levels.

And amazingly, this synchronous effect is achievable in a time period counted in minutes rather than years. Omri Weisman and Orna Zagoory-Sharon explored the impact of artificial oxytocin on the fathering behaviour of thirty-five fathers towards their 5-month-old babies. Oxytocin is one of the few neurochemicals we can manufacture in a lab and, as a result, we can use it to induce bonding behaviours experimentally. In this case, Omri and Orna asked fathers to squirt a dose of either synthetic oxytocin or a placebo – dads didn't know what they were getting – up their nose. This enables the oxytocin to cross from the bloodstream into the brain via the most straightforward route. They then observed the dads interacting with their babies. What they found was that those dads who had received a dose of synthetic oxytocin showed more sensitive and synchronous interactions with their babies. However, the more exciting finding was that despite not having anything squirted up their own noses, the babies' oxytocin levels had also risen in parallel with their dads' – bio-behavioural synchrony in action.

And all dads can work towards achieving this important effect without the aid of a squirt up the nose. I am often asked what the most important things are that a parent can do for their child. I always respond that beyond the need for practical care, the most important thing any parent can do is spend focused, physically close time with their child. Get eye contact, enter into a 'conversation' with sounds or words, take part in reciprocal interactions, shower them with affectionate touch and take the time to tune into their emotional needs so that you respond suitably. If you can do this, and it need only be for five minutes at a time, you are providing your baby with the firm foundations of a secure attachment – and a functioning oxytocin and dopamine system – with which they can go forward and successfully confront life, with all its challenges and rewards.

This close link between parenting style and the development of oxytocin levels in babies also means that the secure bond you develop with your baby has the potential to cross generations. A father's attachment to his own parents has a significant impact on both his baseline oxytocin levels and the sensitivity with which he parents his own child. Dads who perceive their relationship with their parents to be warm and secure have significantly higher oxytocin levels and are more sensitive to their child's needs than fathers who, in contrast, have experienced overly controlling or neglectful childhoods. The environment of a father's upbringing has a profound and very real influence on the way he parents his own children. Parents who have high baseline oxytocin are motivated to practise sensitive parenting, which, in turn, leads to high baseline oxytocin in their offspring, who, in turn, become sensitive parents themselves, and so the cycle continues.

The majority of work on fathering comes from the UK, Australia, the US and, as the location of Ruth Feldman's prolific laboratory, Israel. However, the most powerful evidence for this close association between parenting behaviour and child brain development has recently come from China. In their 2016 study, experimental psychologists Jia Yan, Rachel Han and Peipei Li from Beijing Normal University explored the transmission of parenting styles from grandparent to father and the impact this had on the father's responses to his child's displays of negative emotion.

Yan, Han and Li studied the biological fathers of 172 families from two cities in China. They asked the fathers to complete three questionnaires; one asked them to reflect on their own parenting experience before the age of sixteen, one related to how well they felt they coped with their child's displays of negative emotion and one related to how well they coped with their own negative emotions. The idea was to see whether there was a relationship between how the fathers were parented and how well they coped with their children's more negative emotional outbursts – remember that a secure attachment in childhood leads to a functioning oxytocin system and the ability to cope with life's stressors as an adult. The results were clear. Fathers who had received high levels of care when they were young were adept at dealing with their children's difficult behaviours – they were supportive and ultimately had stronger bonds with their children. In contrast, fathers who reported very controlling parents coped less well with their children's negative emotions. They were overly punitive or dismissive and risked exhibiting controlling or neglectful parenting. The scientists concluded that children who were brought up in controlling environments risked having issues with their abilities to 'emotionally socialize' their own children – that is, teach their children how to process and express their emotions in a healthy way. And as one of the key roles of the father is to build resilience and emotional strength in their child – something we will explore in greater detail in Chapter Ten – these findings have important implications for their children's future mental health and present the possibility that without some sort of intervention, patterns of poor parenting will continue to cross generations.

One aspect of Yan's study that I have not so far mentioned is the fact that the likelihood that the negative parenting behaviours of generation one would pass to generation two was influenced by one aspect of dad's personality – the extent to which he was able to regulate his own emotions. Where he could deal rationally and healthily with his own negative emotions, he was able to overcome the negative experiences of his own childhood and respond to his child's emotional outbursts appropriately and sensitively. However, where he found difficulty in handling his own negative emotions – he lacked the tools to respond effectively or found that his emotion would subsume him, making him unable to control his impulses – here the impact of his childhood experiences were felt in his relationship with his own child.

But the positive that we can take from studies like Yan's and those that we encountered earlier in this chapter that looked at the genetic inheritance of parenting is that having a poor experience of parenting as a child does not necessarily mean that you will yourself fail to be a supportive parent. The relationship is not so clear-cut. Rather, whether or not you overcome your childhood and commence on the path of fatherhood as a 'new man' is dependent on a large number of factors that are both psychological – including your own mental health and personality – and genetic – the extent to which your genes protect you or open you up to risk. But where you may have been dealt a less than ideal genetic or psychological hand, all is not lost. Within the UK, there are several wonderful organizations, details of which are at the end of this book, who under the umbrella of the Parent Infant Project work with parents to overcome their natural tendencies, many of which are the result of their own parenting or traumatic life experiences, to become the most sensitive and wonderful parents. Further, despite the fact that we can recognize a number of factors that contribute to an individual's parenting style, this does not mean we have the 'formula' for successful parenting. And this is because there is always an unknown element: the individual's will to bring about change if needed and work to be the parent they want to be, regardless of the hand life or biology has dealt them.

So, no factor takes the lead in defining who a dad will be – he is, to an extent, a mix of his genes and his experience, but even these two factors do not exist in isolation from each other. A man's own experience of being parented impacts his own practice as a dad, but the relationship is not direct – personality gets in the way. And personality itself is a mix of genetics and experience. It's enough to make your head hurt. But understanding how someone's personality may impact their parenting behaviour is important for explaining the individual differences in fathers that we will observe.

* * *

Imagine the scene. Your toddler is seated in their high chair, ready for lunch. You are under a time pressure, as their morning nap was longer than usual and you need to squeeze lunch in before hightailing it to the doctors for a check-up. You present your child with your carefully thought-out, home-made meal, devised to ensure an optimal nutritional and taste balance. Not for nothing is your kitchen shelf heaving with tomes by the kings and queens of child nutrition. However, your toddler obviously hasn't read the books and is blind to the advantages this healthy meal will confer on him. No, he is less than happy and throws his food on the floor. He then proceeds to attempt an audacious escape from his high chair and make a beeline for the snacks cupboard, where he knows a chocolate biscuit must be lurking. You place him back in his high chair and hurriedly make a sandwich, which you then attempt to feed him by distracting him with a toy and shov-elling it in whenever his mouth is open. Lunch completed, you go to put his shoes on. But he is having none of that and proceeds to throw a full-blown tantrum as you try to quell the beast long enough to make a successful fit between foot and shoe. In the end, you give up and shove on some wellies. Finally, child partially fed and clothed, you begin to make for the door when a familiar smell reaches your nostrils. You exclaim, bundle him up and head for the changing mat.

How do you think this dad would feel? He may take it in his stride, accepting that it is part of the anarchy that is raising a toddler. Or it may leave him feeling like his child is the Antichrist and he the most incompetent parent ever. It will depend in large part on this dad's personality. Remember that there is a general consensus that our personalities are made up of what we call the 'big five' – conscientiousness, extraversion, neuroticism, openness and agreeableness. When we look at personality like this and consider that we are all a varying mixture of all five of these, it becomes clear how our personality can impact the way we parent. Jay Belsky is one of the pioneers of parenting studies. As early as 1984, he argued that how an individual eventually parents is influenced by three key factors. One, their own genetic and psychological resources. Two, the temperament and personality of their child. And three, the external resources of support they can rely upon and sources of stress that they experience. But Jay stated that the most important of these is the first factor and the most vital element of this factor is personality. And this is because a healthy mindset – one high in agreeableness and openness – can act as a buffer against a temperamentally difficult child or an unsupportive marriage or workplace. So, if we are high in neuroticism we may expect and perceive our child to be more badly behaved and ourselves more unsupported, for example, than someone who is predominantly agreeable. Or, if we are high in conscientiousness we may work hard to do a good job as a parent but find the threat to an organized life that children inevitably are tough to take. As a result, we may feel more stressed than someone who is open and comfortable with new experiences and challenges.

My own work with new fathers certainly seems to bear out the influence of a dad's personality on his perception of his fathering experiences. Because I tend to work with fathers during the very early weeks of their journey, I quickly came to understand the influence that a man's personality had on his perception of his birth experience soon after I started researching dads. I remember visiting one dad, Jim, just a couple of weeks after his son, Sean, had been born. As he recounted his experience it became clear that, objectively at least, he had had a pretty traumatic time. His baby had had to be delivered by an emergency caesarean, from which he was by necessity excluded for a significant period of time, and following this his wife had had a life-threatening haemorrhage. He was literally left alone, holding the baby with no idea whether his wife would live. I asked him how he had coped at the time and whether experiencing this had had any long-term impact on his mental health. I expected at least some residual elements of trauma to be present. His reply surprised me and taught me never to assume I knew how someone would cope with any given experience. He said that it had been stressful, but at the time he had reassured himself that he was in the best place and everything that could be done would be. He explained that since then the birth had not troubled him. He was not the sort to ask 'What if?' but was very much of the school of thought that the past is the past and it is best to move forward. Everything had turned out fine, he had been lucky and there was no use in dwelling on what happened. A salutary lesson for me.

A week later, I visited Zac and we discussed his birth experience. Now, these early visits are often quite swift – new dads do not need me taking up any more of their precious down time than is necessary to check everything is okay and take a blood sample – but I spent over an hour with Zac that evening. His baby's birth had been objectively straight-forward – even the dream for some parents. A water birth with minimal intervention had resulted in a beautiful baby boy called Aiden. But Zac was deeply traumatized. He had found watching his wife's pain and his inability to ease it for her almost unbearable and he had been plagued by negative emotion and flashbacks ever since. He was even questioning whether, if they had further children, he would be able to be in the birthing room a second time. Where Jim and Zac differed was their personalities, something I measure at the start of all studies. What to one man is trauma, to another is a situation to endure and then leave behind. As a consequence, it is important to know that as a dad there is no right way to speak of, feel about or cope with your fathering experience – it will be unique to you as a consequence of your individuality.

Personality can continue to impact not only the father–child relationship but the whole family as time progresses. A team of psychologists from the National University of Singapore, led by Ryan Hong, followed 263 fathers for a year following their child's seventh birthday. They wanted to explore whether personality impacted the way each father perceived his child's behaviour and how this related to his parenting behaviour and the extent of family cohesion at the end of the year.

The team found that where a child had no difficulty controlling or expressing his emotions, the father's parenting was characterized by positive support regardless of to what degree his personality could be categorized as neurotic. In contrast, where a child had more difficulty in this area, fathers high in neuroticism coped less well – they tended to overreact, to impose restrictive control in an attempt to curb their child's behaviour and withdraw warmth and support as a punishment. Fathers with high degrees of openness coped well with children who had a bias towards negative feelings – discomfort, fear or anger – perhaps because their openness to new experiences and challenges meant that they did not perceive their child's behaviour to be particularly difficult or stressful – they could go with the flow. Fathers of very active but happy children – trying in their own way, if only on their parent's energy levels – coped better if their personality was dominated by the agreeableness factor, as they could accommodate their child's exuberance. And fathers who were conscientious were able to cope with the challenges of children who had difficulty controlling their emotions and behaviours, perhaps because they benefited from their father's focus on consistent routine and discipline.

Being a dad is a complicated business. There's a lot to learn, to monitor, to focus on and to achieve. And what underlies how the individual man fulfils these tasks is equally as complex. But while you may be the sum of your genetics and your experience, this is not your whole. Individuals do overcome the most neglectful of childhoods and the most risk-laden set of genes to be the most wonderful fathers. Because our destination is not entirely written for us at birth, in the first 1,000 days or even by the totality of our experiences to date. One of the most wonderful things about humans is our ability to reflect on who we are and on who we want to be, and by doing so we get to have some say in our final destination. This may involve you in some work – but with the right help, it is possible. This help may be simply talking about your experiences and difficulties with your partner, family or friends. Or it may need the help of a professional counsellor, who can help you to define, explore and overcome your natural instincts or behaviours. Or it may need more intense help from one of the wonderful organizations listed at the back of this book who help parents come to terms with their life experience and build strong and healthy relationships with their children. But if the will is there, then it is truly possible to be the sort of dad you aspire to be.

PART FOUR

The First Few Weeks

CHAPTER SEVEN

I Love Yah, Baby!

Play, Laughter and Building the Bond

Picture the scene. A father returns from a long day at the office. He opens the door and, before he has even had time to remove his coat, his toddler runs towards him with a squeal of delight, arms outstretched. The father lifts his daughter into his arms and throws her above his head, over and over. Soon, the little girl and her dad are hysterical with laughter. Next, he holds his daughter's hands as she bounces on the sofa, gaining momentum and height with every jump. The dad decides to interrupt this impromptu trampoline session with an energetic bout of tickling before he lifts his daughter up again and aeroplanes her around the room. Finally, exhausted, they both collapse on the sofa in a hug, broad grins stretched across their faces. Daddy is definitely home.

Fathers build deep, profound bonds with their babies that, as we know from previous chapters, can be fundamental to the survival and success of their child. However, as we also now know, beyond changes in his natural baseline levels of oxytocin and testosterone, fathers do not experience the extreme physiological changes associated with pregnancy and childbirth that give mothers a head start in the bonding game. So, what prompts these vital bonds between father and child to develop?

In Chapter Two, we explored the connection that forms between dad and his unborn child, but in this chapter I want to look at the experience of building the arguably more critical bond that develops after birth. For mums, childbirth involves a sea of neurochemicals that are there to start and control the path of labour and provide some respite from the inevitable flood of pain. Luckily for mum, these neurochemicals – oxytocin and beta-endorphin – also have a great side effect: they underpin the bond between a mother and child. Beta-endorphin is a reward chemical in its own right and oxytocin, because of its close relationship with dopamine, also induces feelings of love and euphoria in mum that help her remain bonded to her baby, however tough the long days and nights may be. But although it is undoubtedly an emotional roller coaster for dad, he lacks any experience of the extreme physical and emotional challenges of childbirth, meaning that he must fall back on his physical and verbal interactions with his child to provide the neurochemical kick-start that is required for the all-important bond to form. In the first few days and weeks, finding the opportunity to do this can be somewhat difficult. This period of a baby's life is largely dominated by mum as the source of food and comfort, and fathers can find it difficult to get a look-in. Obviously, they are vital to their new family at this point – supporting mum, dealing with visitors and keeping the domestic show on the road – but finding an activity that defines their exclusive relationship with their child can be hard. Richard's experience of his feelings just after birth are common:

It was difficult to relate to my daughter, Florence, and relate her arrival to me and Sam. I suppose because it was in a medical situation. She got given to me, and then taken to an incubator to do all the stuff, and then given to me again while Sam was getting stitched up, I guess. Obviously, it is a unique experience, it is difficult to characterize. I didn't feel like a father at that point, my mind hadn't quite caught up with what was happening. It was me and Sam in this room with this baby.

Richard, dad to Florence (six months)

In the long-term, building the bond with a child is undoubtedly a rewarding process. However, in the short-term it can be the single biggest source of stress and anxiety for a new father.

For many fathers, like Richard, while the moment of birth brings with it sensations of pride and relief, the expected flood of deep and profound love and attachment is often absent. In the days following birth, this sense of slight separation can be exacerbated by the couple's choice to breastfeed – an intimate behaviour between mum and baby that a dad can support and observe, but not participate in – and by the slow pace of the baby's development, meaning that opportunities to interact are few and far between and rarely result in much recognition from your child. This can be incredibly difficult for a father to handle and can lead him to feel like a 'secondary parent', consigned to the role of chief flower-arranger and chef. Zac's experience echoes that of many new dads:

> I found the first three months certainly the hardest in terms of lack of sleep, not really getting anything back from [my son]. It's just an endless cycle of changing nappies, feeding and burping, crying and so on, but then once you get past that early three months, you start getting things back. Like the first smile is amazing, it's just such a nice feeling, and then you get to the first laugh, and then he reacts to things much better than he did.

Zac, dad to Aidan (six months)

Human babies are astonishingly helpless when born. A newborn human baby can do little more than eat, sleep, cry and be the source of many dirty nappies, a relentless merry-go-round that will be familiar to any new parent. This lack of interpersonal interaction, combined with an as yet undeveloped bond, can make this period unbelievably tough for the new dad. I follow fathers over the long-term and it is not unusual for the apprehensive, excited and well-rested father-to-be of my pre-birth visit to be replaced by an exhausted dad doing a passable impression of the proverbial 'rabbit caught in the headlights' at the two-week post-birth visit. One of my most recent dads experienced a period of self-diagnosed 'baby blues', convinced that his baby didn't like him, as he was unable to comfort her as his wife did. Fathers find themselves trying to fulfil the remit of the involved dad – changing nappies and providing comfort day and night – but without the strong bond that they had envisaged they would feel to fall back on. Combined with very little sleep and a crash course in parenting, where the curriculum can seem to change minute by minute, this is an overwhelming time. But with the passing of weeks, and as the baby's visual acuity improves and allows her to recognize and react to dad with a smile or a giggle, the relationship between dad and baby turns a corner. Play begins to emerge at around three months and the introduction of solid foods at six months provides endless opportunities for fun and involvement, as long as your definition of fun is being liberally covered in puréed apple by a laughing infant.

This gap between the idealized expectation and reality of fathering has been described by some as a case of 'fathering being delayed', and it is certainly true that fathers tend to say that the bond they have with their baby at six months is categorically different in both depth, breadth and complexity than that they felt when their child first emerged. One of the very early pioneers of family studies, Ralph Turner, recognized this phenomenon when, writing in 1970, he argued that the development of the father–infant bond is a two-stage process. The first stage, experienced in most cases at birth and underpinned by oxytocin, relies upon the biological connection between father and child provided by genetic relatedness. The second stage comes much later, is based upon conjoined lives and interactions and is promoted by the much more powerful bonding chemical beta-endorphin, leading to a more profound and much deeper love.

If you are a new dad, this early period of your baby's life can be tough, but there are a few things you can do to ease your anxiety and capture a glimmer of the bond that will, in time, form. It's a good idea to try and find a caretaking duty that is just for you – as we know from Chapter Four, massage is always a good choice both to improve your bond with your baby and to give your mood a boost. Other dads like to get on the reading bandwagon early and read their baby a bedtime story – he or she may not understand the story or even be able to focus on the pictures, but the opportunity to be physically close and to let your baby hear your voice is invaluable. And remember, skin-to-skin is not just for immediately after the birth. Take every opportunity you can to undress your baby (maybe nappy on!) and snuggle them inside your shirt or dressing gown, against your skin. I am told it is the most wonderful experience.

And all first-time fathers agree that they only fulfil their wish to be fully involved, and experience the bond they had hoped for, once the baby is more independent; this is the point at which dads have the opportunity to take on caretaking tasks on an equal footing with their partner and get the endorphins flowing by some serious – and daddy-exclusive – interaction:

> We do interact differently. It's not as if I'm rough with him, but probably my interaction with him, the way I hold him, is different from Sarah and partly that's just if I'm holding him in the air, I can see he is really enjoying it, whereas Sarah would probably be slightly nervous.
>
> *John, dad to Joseph (six months)*

For, once the baby surfaces from the fug of sleep and milk that characterize the early days, one very special and uniquely paternal form of interaction emerges: rough and tumble play.

At first this may be limited to the pulling of silly faces and generation of funny noises to coax a smile or giggle from the still quite tiny baby, but later this interaction will be characterized by a noisy, rough physicality broken by regular periods of hysterical laughter, which often prompt mum to exclaim in alarm. A child is thrown in the air, turned upside down and tickled until it is incapable with laughter; a scenario familiar to us all. It is certainly lots of fun, but this behaviour is also vital to the development and maintenance of the bond between father and child, and it is evolutionarily very ancient. It is clear from comparative studies that many animals play; indeed, it was the observation of this behaviour in our very distant cousins, rats, that prompted scientists to suggest that the function of play extended beyond mere enjoyment to the very underpinnings of infant development. For something to have persisted over such a long period of evolutionary time, it must have an essential link to the survival of our, and many other mammalian, species.

In fact, evolution has played a vital role in making sure that human fathers and babies unconsciously gravitate towards this fun form of interaction. As with all other behaviours that we enjoy – including cuddling, eating pizza and looking at videos of kittens on YouTube – involvement in rough and tumble play stimulates the release of a flood of rewarding chemicals in the brain. The most important of these chemicals for the bond between dad and baby is beta-endorphin, now recognized as the chemical that underpins long-term bonds in humans and other primates.

Beta-endorphin is an astonishing chemical. It's the body's natural painkiller and is fundamental to the operation of many of the body's vital functions, including digestion and the regulation of the cardiovascular and renal systems. But it is within the brain that the power of this chemical is really apparent. Beta-endorphin receptors are located in all the brain's key areas, including at the core of the brain within the limbic system and on the outer surface within the neo-cortex. This means it has a role in the experience of the most basic of emotions, including fear and love, and in the more considered and cognitively more demanding decisions of the conscious neocortex, which include the ability to navigate our socially and technologically complex modern world. It is this wide-ranging brief that secures beta-endorphin its place as the king of bonding chemicals, because it is capable of supporting all the many subtle nuances of human relationships. And it is addictive! It is the body's natural opiate, so once someone has experienced an interaction that causes a release of this chemical, they will keep on returning for more. They are addicted to the wonderful feelings of warmth, closeness, euphoria and happiness that it engenders. And a wide range of behavioural interactions can feed this addiction, including laughter:

I seem to be able to get him to laugh very, very easily, kind of fits of laughter, and a lot of it is just jumping around and scaring him. Stuff that my wife would never think of doing but that is something that we do between us, and it's some-thing that's just me and him. I am the only person who can get him to laugh pretty much on cue. [There's a] pride in enjoying it, there is that little link there that I never expected to happen that quickly at all.

Will, dad to Christopher (six months)

We know that humans experience endorphin hits when they touch each other, when they laugh and when they sing and dance. Indeed, my own research group at Oxford, headed by Professor Robin Dunbar, has pioneered research that has shown that human relationships, from the simple twosome to the chanting football crowd, are bonded by activities that promote beta-endorphin release. And if these activities can be synchronous, such as the strokes of a rowing eight, the singing of the choir or the laughter of the audience at a comedy show, so much the better.

It is only very recently that we have obtained conclusive proof that endorphins also lie at the heart of the bond between parent and child. In her 2016 paper published in *Brain, Behavior, and Immunity*, Adi Ulmer-Yaniv and her colleagues explored the release of beta-endorphin, oxytocin and interleukin-6 – a new chemical to add to our repertoire, which is implicated in the stress immune response – in the formation of bonds between lovers and between parents and their children. Ulmer-Yaniv argued that a combination of the body's affiliation, reward and stress systems is involved in the development of attachment in these closely bonded relationships. Oxytocin lowers the inhibitions to forming relationships (affiliation), beta-endorphin provides an addictive reward and interleukin-6 represents the inevitable stress associated with forming a new bond – we all remember the uncertainty surrounding our first love. Her study involved twenty-five heterosexual couples who were in a new relationship, 115 first-time mums and dads of 4–6-month-old babies and twenty-five single people who acted as a control. She took blood samples from all her subjects and then asked those in relationships to carry out an interaction in their couples. For mums and dads, that was playing with their baby for ten minutes, while romantic couples had to plan 'the best day ever' to spend together. Researchers noted to what extent the subjects displayed a range of positive bonding behaviours – shared gaze, facial emotion, vocalizations and touch – and to what extent they were synchronous. What they found was that in those relationships where new bonds were being formed – that's parent to baby and between lovers – levels of all three chemicals were significantly higher than in the singles group. Further, new parents had higher levels of beta-endorphin and interleukin-6 than the new lovers, whereas the levels of oxytocin were higher in the new lover group. What does all this mean? It means that we have conclusive evidence that beta-endorphin is the key chemical underpinning the long-term bond between baby and parent, that becoming a parent is more stressful than falling in love (!) and that oxytocin, while significant particularly in the short-term, hence its high levels at the start of the lovers' relationship, does not act alone to bond parent to child. Indeed, Ulmer-Yaniv found that the relationship between the three chemicals is at its peak during this frenzy of new bond formation. And that frenzy is the same whether you are a dad or a mum. Beta-endorphin really is the chemical of parental love.

It should now be clear why rough and tumble play is essential to forming the bond between dad and baby, and why it is the perfect interaction to cause a big beta-endorphin rush. With its overt physicality and laughter and its requirement that the players synchronize their behaviour for the best play experience – no good launching yourself into the air with no one to catch you – it is the perfect prompt for this essential chemical to be released. But why is it fathers who are the predominant exhibitors of this behaviour? And why has research repeatedly shown that children show a preference for playing with their dads rather than their mums? The answer lies in the wonderful synchrony of brain development that has been positively selected for in parents and their offspring to ensure that bonds develop and that the child experiences the best developmental environment in which to grow up.

In another pioneering study, Ruth Feldman observed Israeli mothers and fathers during fifteen-minute periods of play and interaction with their 4–6-month-old infants. She took samples of saliva and blood before and after these sessions from both parents and found, in both cases, that their levels of oxytocin rose following interaction with their baby. However, there was a crucial difference between fathers and mothers in the nature of the interaction that produced the most significant spike in oxytocin levels. For the mothers, the spike was prompted by interactions characterized by affectionate care but not play – cuddling, stroking and soft vocalization. For the fathers, the reverse was true: the spike was caused by rough and tumble play and not affectionate care, despite the fathers displaying both types of behaviour. As we will see later in this chapter, the role of play buddy is developmentally vital to a child, so evolution has fitted fathers to take it on by ensuring that it is associated with a special reward; fathers have a preference for the behaviour that gives them the biggest reward. Such a conclusion is supported by the finding that if you squirt oxytocin up a father's nose before he interacts with his baby – yes, being a scientist can be an odd day job – his play behaviour becomes even more boisterous and all-consuming, but there is no increase in his nurturing behaviour.

So, we have an explanation for the father's almost automatic desire to play with his child. But what of the child? Well, again, for the baby there seems to be a relationship between who you choose to play with and the size of the neurochemical reward you receive. As the parents get a behaviour-specific boost, so the child mirrors this with his own oxytocin levels. So, an infant will get an oxytocin boost from the affectionate care of his mother and from the playful behaviour of his father. And this is as a consequence, once more, of that amazing neurochemical phenomenon, bio-behavioural synchrony. As with the essential bond between expectant parents, this is as fundamental to the healthy development of the bond between the parent and child. Because much of this interaction between parent and child begins during the first year of life, when a human baby's brain is rapidly growing and forming, this leads to the development of neurochemical synchrony between preferred partners. And as a result, the preferred partner for play is dad and for nurture, mum. This finding leads me to two clear conclusions. First, that play is the method by which Western fathers develop and underpin their profound bond with their children and, second, that the role division we see between mothers and fathers is driven to an extent by biology and an evolutionary drive that aims to provide the optimal developmental environment for the child.

However, the story of play is not one of pure biological hardwiring. The eagle-eyed among you may have noticed the insertion of the word 'Western' in the preceding sentence.

For it is only Western fathers who are seen to engage in *signif-icant* amounts of rough and tumble play with their children. Indeed, if we consider the Congolese Aka father that we encountered in Chapter Five, this paragon of involved, hands-on fathering rarely plays with his children, choosing instead to keep them in close physical proximity at all times and entertaining them with stories and songs. If play is the mech-anism that underpins bonding in Western fathers, why is it not seen to the same extent in non-Western families, where the bond between father and child is undoubtedly just as strong? It is all a matter of time. Western fathers are often absent for a significant period of their child's day, often working in an environment that is separate to the home. This means that the time they have available to build and maintain their bond is much reduced. Rough and tumble play is often described as quite extreme in both physicality and volume, and it is within this lack of reserve that its effectiveness lies. Play provides Western fathers with a quick and efficient mechanism for developing a bond with their child. Beta-endorphin is a pow-erful and addictive chemical, and the speed of play means that its participants must learn to quickly read another's intentions and emotions to avoid upset, so it is a fast-track mechanism for getting to know someone. In a time-poor world, this is vital to ensure fathers and babies develop their bond. In contrast, the fathers of the Aka take their children with them everywhere, when they hunt and when they socialize, so they have all the time in the world to both be in contact, leading to oxytocin and beta-endorphin release, and to get to know each other's characters.

The delay in developing the connection with your child

can be a difficult issue for the modern father, prepared as he is to fully co-parent from day one. Speaking for myself, I feel we owe it to fathers to help them manage their expectations regarding this period in their lives. It would be wonderful if midwives, health visitors and antenatal educators could explain to dads that their relationship with their child is as vital and unique as that between mother and child, but that it develops at a different pace and via a different mechanism. That by comparing yourself to the mother as the 'gold standard', you are at risk of setting yourself up to fail. Because, dads, you are not male mothers. Rather you are an equally vital but different player in your child's world and if you are patient, invest your time and energy – critically, your tickling, bouncing and running energy – and do not lose heart, you will develop the most profound and rewarding relationship with your child.

As we know from Chapter Two, the relationship between a parent and child is not just a bond, it is an attachment. But while the prenatal attachment is largely driven by dad or mum, the attachment after birth involves baby's behavioural and emotional input too. All mammalian babies form attachment relationships with their mothers, but humans are one of the very few mammals where a baby forms this intense reciprocal relationship with dad.

You start out with this one-way street where you're giving a lot, and that's fine, I went into it knowing that was going to be the case and now I am reaping the benefits a thousand-fold of what I put into it. But I would say, in the last couple of months [my son] has started now to give back into the relationship as well and he's now able to smile, he is interacting and grabbing and pulling on my hair, all of these sorts of things, and that's a lot of fun.

Jim, dad to Sean (six months)

For many decades, it was felt that the only relationship of concern with respect to the well-being of the child was that between mother and child and, as such, tools for assessing the father–infant bond were deemed to be surplus to requirements. It is only very recently, due to the growing evidence that a father's relationship with his child *can* have a profound effect on their development, that this gap in our academic arsenal has been filled. We met one of the pioneers of this area, John Condon of Flinders University in Adelaide, Australia, in Chapter Two. Over the past decade, he and his team have developed measures that assess the attachment between father and baby both before and after birth. Recognizing that the relationship between father and child was fundamentally different both in type and function than that between mother and child, they were the first to argue for dad-specific measures. Until this point, and as is still disappointingly the case in postnatal mental health assessment, measures designed for mothers were applied in a wholesale manner to fathers, making any reliable diagnosis difficult.

But using the transcripts of numerous interviews with fathers that explored the dad–baby bond, John was able to come up with a uniquely dad-focused definition of this crucial connection, based on three distinct areas of emotion and behaviour. These were patience and tolerance, pleasure in interaction, and affection and pride. He found that if, as a dad, you are securely attached to your baby, you won't report significant boredom or irritability – though have no doubt, it will have been there – you will experience pleasure and satisfaction and a sense of competency, and describe a background feeling of warmth and pride when interacting with your children. The extent to which you perform these behaviours or experience these emotions will change between the baby's sixth month and first birthday. At six months, being a tolerant dad appears to be more important than experiencing pleasure – the survival approach – but this pattern is reversed at twelve months, mirroring the change in fathering experience that both I and other researchers have observed in the fathers we study. As your baby develops and becomes more and more involved in life, so the need for tolerance subsides and the pleasure of play and two-way communication comes to the fore. Being a dad starts to become truly enjoyable.

The ability of a father to attach securely to his child is decided, in part, during the dad's own early childhood. As I have mentioned in earlier chapters, the bond a baby builds with his parents occurs at the same time as areas of the brain critical to social behaviours are forming, and much of what a man knows about fathering, consciously and unconsciously, he inherits or learns from his parents. As a consequence, dysfunctional parenting relationships and behaviours can cross generations. But there is hope for those fathers who wish to choose a different parenting path to that of their own parents. As our knowledge of the unique post-birth father–infant attachment grows, we are identifying more and more factors that affect the success or otherwise of this relationship. We have found that dads seem to be strongly affected by their immediate environment, in particular the nature of their relationship; the support for their role from their partner and the health of their relationship with him or her both have a profound effect on how well he attaches to his child. In addition, his mental health, the temperament of his baby – angelic, boisterous or fussy – and his general sense of competency as a parent may also be highly significant factors.

In a recent study, a team from Monash University in Melbourne, Australia, tried to tease apart these factors to see if one had a greater influence than any other on the strength of the bond between father and baby. Led by developmental psychologist Karen Wynter, it measured the strength of attachment between dad and baby at four weeks and six months after birth. At the same time, they asked the 270 fathers to complete a barrage of questionnaires related to their mental health, the extent to which they had a vulnerable personality, the characteristics of their child and the health of their relationship with, and the support they received from, their partner. What they found was that dads who had the weakest attachments to their children were more likely to suffer from mental ill health, have more vulnerable personalities – that is lacked assertiveness and were oversensitive to criticism – and were on the receiving end of less support and more criticism of their fathering from their partner. So, it would appear that a number of factors do play a role in how well a man can bond to his child, both external and internal. But one of the long-held assumptions regarding parent–infant bonding wasn't supported – that difficult children are harder to bond with. The nature of the child's temperament had no influence on how well the father developed his bond with him or her. Indeed, as we explored in the last chapter, some fathers – those with agreeable and open personalities most notably – may thrive on the opportunity to bond with a more challenging child.

The issues of identity that I explored in Chapter Three also appear to have a powerful influence on the strength of bond between father and child. In their 2010 study of expectant first-time fathers, Cherine Habib and Sandra Lancaster found that fathers who felt that being an equal caregiver to their child was a key aspect of their new identity went on to exhibit stronger attachment to their newborn than those who prioritized a role as helper – the classic 'secondary parent' – or breadwinner. What is key for those of us who work with fathers is that many of these studies focus on the *prenatal* or very early post-birth period, meaning that, as I have already said in Chapter Three, we can predict which fathers may struggle to form the vital attachment to their child before their baby is born or very soon after. Once identified, these dads and their partners can be offered support and guidance to help them to develop a healthier environment – work that focuses on building a supportive relationship with their partner, assessing their mental health and teaching practical skills to underpin their sense of competency as a dad. And, of course, helping them to understand that at the very root of the relationship between a father and his baby are those very basic human behaviours of touch and laughter, talking and singing. So, it is about freeing the father to get in touch with his inner child and to relate to his baby on his or her level.

While it is clearly the case that both mum and dad form deep attachment relationships with their children, it is still the case that in many traditional Western families the mother forms the primary attachment figure for the child, largely as a consequence of the father's need to earn money away from the home. However, in some cases, even with the restrictions on contact time that work imposes, fathers can and do act as the primary attachment figure for their children.

In their 2010 study of child-to-father attachment, Todd Goodsell and Jaren Meldrum of the University of Utah, in the US, used interviews with expectant mothers to explore their relationships with their fathers. They focused on four mothers in particular, who had secure attachments to their fathers but insecure attachments to their own mothers. They wanted to explore the circumstances of the family structure that led to this phenomenon and the skills and inputs that the father brought to their relationship. In all cases, mum was around and both mum and dad were employed part- or full-time, so the attachment between father and child could not be the consequence of a primary caretaking father.

What they found was that these fathers, rather like our primary caretaking gay dads, fulfilled the range of required roles – nurturer, caretaker, wage-earner, playmate and teacher – to ensure that, in the absence of a healthy attachment between mother and daughter, all the developmental and survival bases were covered. Among the group of dads they heard about, Todd and Jaren point to 'examples of versatile dads' who act as the primary supporter at cheerleading meets and community activities; as the source of counsel in dating and courtship; as the more 'caring' and 'sympathetic' parent; as the one more prone to give hugs, verbal affection and encouragement; as the moral and academic teacher; as the listener; and even handling such situations as his daughter's first menstruation.

Even during that most male of dad-instigated activities, rough and tumble play, daughters reported that their fathers used sessions to offer advice, voice their opinions and even to teach. These fathers were able to build this attachment to their children despite being at work for the majority of the day, showing us that proximity is not the most important factor when building a relationship with your child. Reassuring news for those of us who juggle work and home life against a constant, low-level noise of guilt.

But why were these dads so prominent in their children's lives? In some cases, they were compensating for a mother who could not or would not show affection to her children. In others, perhaps there was a clash of personalities between mother and child, or the child perceived that their mother was not sufficiently nurturing, causing the child to focus on their father, to whom they may have greater affinity in personality and outlook. But what this study shows us is that the attachment between father and child is as deep, profound and multifaceted as that between mother and child. It is an essential source of both care and affection but also, critically, the practical, emotional and experiential knowledge that will form the strong foundation for a successful life.

* * *

I started this chapter with rough and tumble play, and it is with rough and tumble play we end. For it is in this form of play that we see the key survival-related function of father–child attachment. Play is fun – the shrieks of laughter and ebullient energy are testament to this. But play can also be scary – it requires a fine understanding of the other person's intentions and limits, and a high level of trust. In this, it is much the same as the new friendship or acquaintance. We are tempted by the potential for enjoyment and intimacy – and that all-important endorphin hit – but we are fearful of rejection and emotional pain. In playing with their children, Western fathers are not only cementing their bond but doing something that is equally vital to their survival. They are preparing them for life in our rough, tough social world. Humans need to cooperate with each other to survive – to raise our children, to learn the skills to ultimately be financially independent and to ensure we have the basic resources for life: food, water and shelter. Rough and tumble play enables the child to explore the skills required for this world from a secure base – they can always return to dad for a reassuring hug. I will talk more about this role when we consider the role of the father as teacher in Chapter Nine and in child development in Chapter Ten but, as we know from John Condon's work, researchers are increasingly aware that the nature of the attachment between father and child is categorically different to that between mother and child. Karin and Klaus Grossmann have suggested that while the mother–child attachment is characterized by security in the relationship, based on affectionate care and nurturing, the father-to-infant attachment is characterized by a secure relationship *and* secure exploration. Indeed, developmental psychologist Daniel Paquette from the University of Montreal, Canada, conceives of the relationship between father and child as being one of activation rather than attachment. He argues that this close bond allows the child to have the confidence to explore unusual environments, to use their initiative and take risks, to be self-sufficient and confident in the presence of strangers. The father–child relationship is the source of individuality and autonomy and, ultimately, success.

And this striking difference in attachments is reflected in the way we explore how a child relates to his or her attachment figure. When we want to understand the relationship between a baby and its mother, there is no use getting the clipboard out and delivering a questionnaire – that way lies an entertained baby but a lot of ripped paper and a chewed pen. We use a behavioural scenario instead. It is called The Strange Situation and was first created by developmental psychologist Mary Ainsworth in the 1970s. It uses a sequence of interactions between the baby, its mother and a stranger (usually a researcher) to explore how well the child is attached to their mother. By observing how the child interacts with the stranger, both accompanied and unaccompanied by their mother, and how they behave when reunited with their mother following a period of separation, the extent to which the child is securely attached can be assessed. But those of us who work with fathers recognized that, while of course fathers nurture their children, the fact that few are the primary carer and that the nature of interaction between dads and their children is different, this scenario was not able to capture the unique bond between dad and child from the child's perspective. What the child looked for from their relationship with their dad was different. So, Daniel Paquette and his colleague Marc Bigras developed The Risky Situation – there's a clue about its focus in the title. In this scenario the child, usually aged between twelve and eighteen months, is presented with two apparently challenging situations. A social risk – as represented by a stranger – and a physical risk – a set of stairs. And the way in which a child interacts with the stranger and the stairs gives us a strong indication of the nature of their attachment to their dad.

The classification of a child's attachment to their parent produces three distinct categories of attachment behaviour – secure, anxious or ambivalent, and avoidant. Secure children are confident in the relationship they have with their carer, are able to be soothed by them and, while distressed on separation, they are capable of self-soothing because they feel safe in the knowledge that if their carer leaves they will return. Anxious children worry that their carer will leave them and, as such, find it difficult to be separated from them and are nervous of taking risks. Avoidant children are very independent emotionally and physically from their carer. They display no expectation that the carer will help or soothe them and show no distress on separation from them. Often, they will be seen to take quite extreme physical risks.

In Daniel and Marc's test, children who are securely attached will explore the environment and interact with the stranger confidently but with a sensible level of risk and will obey any rules their father has set them. In contrast, those who are anxiously attached will remain in close physical proximity to their dad and not explore either the stranger or the stairs. Avoidant children are reckless in their exploration of both stranger and stairs and don't obey the rules their father has set them. By understanding the very different bond between father and child, Paquette and Bigras were able to develop a scenario that encompassed this vital and complex relationship in one easy test.

At the academic level, we know that the bond between father and baby is fundamental to the child's development, the healthy functioning of the family and the stability of society. But at the personal level, it is about the profound, reciprocated love between parent and child. For expectant fathers, it lies at the very centre of their daydreams about their life with their future child and for that reason alone, it requires our attention. If you are an expectant or new dad, then remember this: there is no right way to feel when your baby is born or when you first meet your adopted child, and while some dads may feel a rush of profound and deep love, for the majority, like Adrian, who has shared his story, this is not their experience.

> Funnily enough, all the way through it was always like, 'Adrian will be the naturally bonded one. He'll be the one who takes the time off, because he is child-friendly and he is the nurturer.' But actually, when it got to going to meet [our daughter] for the first time, Noah was the cool one who got down and played with her, and I just sat on the sofa, a bit freaked out by it.
>
> *Adrian, dad to Judy (seven)*

Adrian's experience will be very familiar to many dads. But I can reassure you that Adrian went on to develop a strong and secure attachment to Judy. Meeting your baby or child can be a stressful and slightly alienating time, as you come to terms with this new being who has come into your family and fundamentally rewritten its structure and operation. We know now that the bond will take time and in all likelihood will not truly begin to develop until you are able to have two-way interactions with your child, to really get to know their personality and for them to get to know yours. But there are many ways you can help this special bond grow – carving out special one-on-one time, making a caretaking activity exclusively yours, ensuring that laughter and touch lie at the centre of your interactions, and dusting off your best play moves. Try to be comfortable with the pace. It will come. And remember the bond your partner develops with your child – mum or fellow father – will be different to yours because you are different people and you may have different roles. Try not to compare yourself or compete. There is no gold standard. What a child ultimately needs is a secure attachment with their dad to enable them to feel safe venturing out into the world and experiencing life – the good bits and the bad bits – with the toolkit that you will have furnished them with and secure in the knowledge that you are there, their rock, to whom they will always be able to return for care and reassurance.

CHAPTER EIGHT

And Two Become Three (or Four, or Five . . .)

Parents' Roles and Relationships

A mum and a dad sit beside each other on a sofa, eyes glued to their television screen. On the screen is a video of a child, a little girl, their daughter. She is playing in a garden on a warm, sunny day. As the parents watch the screen, their faces are animated with emotion. The little girl is in her own world of imaginary play. They share a knowing look and a smile as they watch their child run and laugh with abandon. A glimmer of concern and anxiety flickers across the mother's face as her child navigates the rope net on the climbing frame, her grip on the ropes slipping suddenly, while the father's face glows with pride as he observes his child's athleticism and bravery. Their child's hysterical laughter as she chases a harassed-looking pigeon across the lawn leads to a similar burst of laughter from her parents as they are taken up in her moment of joy. This is a scene repeated in homes across the land and we could argue that the reactions we see, split as they are along sex lines, are wholly typical.

In this chapter, I want to expand our focus a little to move beyond just dad and consider the family. To explore how both parents can work together to provide a child with all he or she needs to develop, but also to understand how adding a baby (or two, or three . . .) can have an impact on a relationship. We'll consider the best way to make sure this is a happy transition for everyone. And I will show you the profoundly different way that mum and dad conceive of their family and the relationships within it, which can help us understand why difficulties in the parenting relationship have a significantly more negative impact on dad and his family relationships than anyone else.

We may joke about the difference in parenting styles between men and women – a well-worn cliché given full run-out in numerous sitcoms and movies – but what we are observing here are the results of half a million years of brain evolution, with the ultimate aim of producing a team that is ideally adapted to provide the best environment for raising a child. Not all children emerge into the world as members of a nuclear family – heterosexual or gay. But for those that do, their arrival can have a profound effect on both parents' brains, biology and psychology.

A distinction they see in us . . . is the way we do discipline. I tend to be the one more likely to become quickly angry, whereas Sarah is more balanced, able to reason with them. What would they come to me for? Maybe it's around the things I enjoy, the things I like doing with them, so if they want a bike ride they will come to me. Sarah tends to do more creative things with them; I come home and there are paints and crayons [and I think], *Ooh, looks like hard work.*

John, dad to Joseph (four) and Leo (two)

179

John's observation is one I hear with reasonable regularity. We learnt in Chapter Two that during pregnancy the baseline levels of oxytocin of parents-to-be are synchronized. It is believed that this wonder of biology – triggered by the cohabiting couple's close behavioural and physiological bond – occurs to ensure the relationship between the couple is strong and that as parents they will speak and act as one; crucial if they want to maintain some semblance of control and provide the stable foundation that their child will need. But evolution hates redundancy – the idea that two people will carry out a survival-critical behaviour when it only requires one to do so. Energy is finite, and the job of raising a human child is complex. Evolution is loath to make both parents fulfil a task when one could be freed up to achieve a different and equally vital parenting goal. As a consequence, this level of hormonal synchrony is not necessarily mirrored by behavioural synchrony. Of course, we know this. Even among those most equal of parents, the Aka of the Congo in Africa, there are still roles that are distinct to mum and dad – dad for co-sleeping, mum for feeding. In the West, it is generally the case that in traditional family set-ups, dads play and mums nurture. Dads push developmental boundaries and mums plan activity timetables. Dads fix broken toys and buy games consoles, mums handle the baking, painting and sticking, just like John's wife. We know from Chapter Seven that dads get a peak in oxytocin when playing with their child, while for mums this chemical rush is reserved for caring behaviours. The brain has evolved to ensure that the parents favour doing very different but equally vital activities with their children – and as such, all the bases are covered by the parenting team.

And this neurochemical split is mirrored by a corresponding split in brain activity.

In 2012, fifteen pairs of heterosexual parents of 6-month-old babies volunteered to be placed in a fMRI scanner and have their brain activity assessed while they watched videos of their children playing. Israeli psychologist Shir Atzil wanted to see whether the behavioural and neurochemical differences we see between dads and mums are reflected in differences in their brain activity when involved in a child-centred activity. What she hoped to see was synchrony in some areas of the brain, reflecting the skills and behaviours that all parents need to exhibit to build a secure attachment, but asynchrony in others, reflecting the distinct behavioural differences between the members of the parenting team. And her wishes were granted. While viewing the video of their child playing, both mums and dads showed activity in the areas of the brain linked to empathy and mentalizing. Mentalizing is the ability to read and understand the thoughts and feelings of another person – to place yourself in their shoes. It is essential if you want to manipulate someone, or lie or cheat, as it allows you to second-guess their next move. But it is also essential if you are to care for someone, for it allows you to feel what they feel, respond appropriately and anticipate what they may need next. This ability is fundamental to a secure attachment between parent and child, and the activity patterns in the brains of both parents show us that both mum and dad have the neural capability to build a strong attachment to their child.

But in other areas of the brain, there was a distinct difference between the sexes. In the brains of the mothers, the ancient centre, known as the limbic system, was the most active. Within this area, at the very core of the brain, lie the brain systems associated with emotion. The fact that they are more active in mothers than fathers may reflect the key characteristics of mothering – giving affection and nurturing. One area of the limbic system, the amygdala, was particularly active. This small structure detects, and causes a reaction to, risk, suggesting that as well as caring for their child, a mother is constantly monitoring the environment for any potential threats – that slippery rope ladder in the introduction to this chapter being one. In contrast, in the father's brain it was the neocortex that was set alight – the outer, deeply riven surface of the brain. In particular, the areas associated with social cognition – responsible for enabling someone to handle complex thoughts and tasks and make plans. This may reflect the special responsibility a father takes for teaching and encouraging his child to strive towards independence above and beyond that carried out by mum. When viewing the video of his playing child, the father is assessing her abilities and planning the next step in pushing her developmental boundaries. Furthermore, the fact that a father's activity is located in this brain structure – the site of our species' advanced intelligence and abilities – reflects the innate flexibility of the dad's role.

We know from Chapter Five that the power and value of the fathering role lies in great part with his ability to respond quickly to environmental changes to ensure the survival of his offspring. To do this, you have to be intellectually quick-thinking – hence a father engages his neocortex. What is also interesting is that the locations of these intense activations – the ancient brain core in mothers and relatively new outer neocortex in fathers – reflects the different evolutionary time points of the emergence of these roles. Mothering is as old as time, present in the earliest reptiles, whereas we know that human fatherhood is only 500,000 years old at best, meaning its skills are hard-wired into the newest area of the brain.

Let's be clear, Shir's results do not mean that fathers never care and mothers never teach – we all know this not to be true. Fathers showed activation in the limbic area and mothers in the neocortex, but the extent of this activity was much less as compared to their opposite-sex partner. To avoid redundancy, evolution has shaped the brains of mothers and fathers to focus on different aspects of their child's needs to ensure that, together, they meet all her developmental needs. And remember that the same is true for the gay parenting team; the primary caretaking dad shows activation in both regions of the brain. Within the nuclear family, evolution has ensured that, regardless of parental sexuality, a child is cared for by the perfect parenting team.

* * *

Both Deb and myself said, [for the] first month or so, we felt like Anna wasn't ours, wasn't our baby; it was weird, and it was only a few months in that you started to say, 'It's our little ball of fun.' And only really recently when she has started to get a little character do you really think, *This is my daughter and this is who I am going to be looking after, watch grow and stuff like that.* So, it took a good few weeks, if not months, to really realize you have this baby for the next . . . [however many years].

Steve, dad to Anna (six months)

Pregnancy is one of the very few periods in our life that has a firmly defined beginning and end. In most cases this allows parents nine solid months in which to prepare themselves for the whirlwind of parenthood. Obviously, this means that there is time to do all the essential practical jobs and engage in some serious equipment shopping, but there is also time to focus on the relationship between mum and dad. Unfortunately, this is often an area of preparation that gets overlooked – it is rarely the focus of antenatal classes and not something that most parents-to-be take much time to discuss. But if you think of it using the analogy beloved of human resources managers, that of the effective workplace team, before you are parents, you are a team of two and have gone through the sometimes rocky stages of team-building that mean that, hopefully, you have reached a happy equilibrium and rub along together well. However, having a baby is adding another member to that team and at a time when you both may have very few physical and mental resources to fall back on – this can result in a considerable 'storm', as everyone comes to terms with their new place in the order. The couple are being asked to work together, carrying out tasks that neither of them initially know how to start, let alone complete, with a new boss who is not terribly good at communicating what he or she needs beyond screaming at them. Sounds stressful, doesn't it? Hopefully it is clear why, to cope with this new dynamic, it is a good idea to try to make the relationship between the parents as strong and healthy as it can possibly be *before* baby is added to the mix.

We know that, for both mum and dad, how positive they find the experience of becoming a parent is strongly linked to how satisfied they are with their relationship. That is, the more cohesive, consensual and affectionate the relationship, the more satisfied the individual is with their partner and the more they rate becoming a parent as a positive experience. In particular, new parents rate their relationship highly if three criteria are met. Firstly, how mutually supportive and encouraging their partner is regarding their parenting role. Secondly, how aligned their ideas are about co-parenting and how happy they are with the way the baby-related chores are divided up. And, thirdly, the temperament and developmental stage of their baby. It is truly the case that life does become easier as your baby develops and can communicate their needs effectively and can meet some of these needs, such as feeding, themselves. This in turn makes parents less stressed and, hopefully, their relationship more stable. But beyond these jointly shared issues, there are some factors that are more important to dad than to mum and these mostly centre on the temperament of the baby and, more relevant here, the support dad receives from mum for his role as a father.

Maternal gatekeeping is the term given to beliefs, attitudes and behaviours that exclude the father from spending time with his child. In its most extreme version it only occurs at low frequencies within the global population, but elements of it can be seen in a significant number of parental relationships where conflict is a regular occurrence. It is most often seen in separated or divorcing couples, but also exists within families where the parents cohabit. It can be caused by, and be the cause of, marital difficulty, as the mother uses access to the child as a weapon in her disagreements with her partner, which leads to instability in the family and further conflict. It is important to recognize, because it has serious consequences for the marital relationship, the relationship between father and child and the development of the child. Mothers who practise maternal gatekeeping tend to be overly and publicly critical of their partner's parenting style. They tend to undermine his attempts at discipline and set unachievable criteria for allowing him to spend time with his child. They control all of the child's activities and scheduling and, believing that mothers make the best carers, find it very hard to relinquish any of the care of the child to anyone else. Ultimately, they believe that the father is very much an assistant rather than an equal in the parenting project – they, as the mother, are the boss.

In their study of 365 Mexican American and European American families, a team of psychologists and sociologists from a number of American universities, led by Matthew Stevenson, explored both the causes of gatekeeping and the impact it had on the relationship between father and adolescent child and the adolescent child's sense of importance – their self-esteem. They found that, irrespective of ethnicity or socio-economic group, an increase in marital problems – such as volatility, criticism, jealousy or infidelity – led to an increase in maternal gatekeeping beliefs in the mother. This in turn meant that fathers spent less time with their children, regardless of the gender of the child. The impact of this on the child was a sense that they did not matter or mattered less to their father than they previously had. As such feelings lead to increases in negative self-absorption and inability to control emotions, these are worrying consequences for the children within these families.

Luckily, many fathers won't experience maternal gatekeeping in their relationship with their partner. But the behaviours and mental health of all fathers are influenced by how their partners behave towards them in their role as a father. Where partners are encouraging and support the father in their role and actively enable the father to have time with his child, the risk of the father's poor mental health decreases and the ease with which he adopts his new identity increases. And this has positive consequences for the bond he can build with his child. In their 2014 study, a joint team from the University of Sussex and City University London in the UK, led by Ylva Parfitt, followed a group of parents-to-be as they transitioned to parenthood. During pregnancy, seventy-two women and sixty-six of their male partners (not all the dads wanted to take part) were asked about their mental health and their degree of satisfaction with their relationship. The team then waited for babies to be born and repeated these measures for all when their babies were three and fifteen months old, with the addition of a measure that assessed the baby's temperament. Two valuable conclusions were drawn. Firstly, for both parents, how strong the bond was between them and their baby was most significantly affected by how they had rated their relationships during pregnancy, meaning that we can get a good handle on the quality of the future relationship between parent and child by assessing their interactions with their partner. Secondly, this link between relationship satisfaction and the strength of the bond between baby and parent was still the case for men at the fifteen-month mark, in combination with his level of mental health, whereas, for the mums, the key factor impacting their relationship with their child at this point was only his or her temperament. The influence of the state of the parenting relationship appeared to be more influential for a longer period of time on the relationship between dad and baby than mum and baby. What this means for parents is that working on your relationship during pregnancy to make sure it is the healthiest it can be will make bonding with your child easier and that, particularly for dad, keeping half an eye on your relationship once baby is there is important. Seek out those willing babysitters, take some time to be a couple and try to make sure baby isn't your sole topic of conversation, however tempting it may be.

> [It's] been almost like our relationship is on holiday for a moment, so I wouldn't say we don't have a relationship, but it is very different in terms of what we talk about every day. It is obviously focused more on our baby at the moment. The first thing I get when I walk in the door is, 'Do you know how many times he ate this?' 'He did that.' 'This was in his nappy.' That is the daily report. It has changed our dynamic quite a bit and I wouldn't say that's a bad thing, it's just part of the next stage for us and at some point I hope we move back to more of an intimate setting ... [where] the two of us can sit down and chat about something other than nappies.
>
> *Jim, dad to Sean (six months)*

It is clear from previous chapters that fathers and mothers experience the transition to parenthood – that is, the period of time it takes to feel comfortable and competent as a parent – very differently. It is not entirely clear why this might be, but

I could suggest that it is linked to the longer period required for a father to bond with his child, as we explored in Chapter Seven, and the fact that the current status of the father in Western families is still that of the secondary parent. Fathers are still the most likely parent to head out to work while mum takes on most of the primary care. As a result, dad's time with his child is limited to evenings, weekends and the annual family holiday. This means fathers have less time to practise their new-found parenting skills and achieve the level of competence that will allow them to feel comfortable inhabiting their new role.

All of these differences between mum and dad need to be accommodated within this new parental relationship, and if this is not achieved via constructive rather than destructive communication – taking time to explore feelings about parenthood, arriving at a joint co-parenting plan, avoiding judgement and criticism, taking care to remain supportive of each other – the quality of the marital relationship and the cohesiveness of the family will diminish.

Once baby has arrived, the new family will exist at three levels of organization: the individual, the couples (teams of two: mum and dad, baby and dad, baby and mum) and the family (mum, dad and baby). Research by Ilanit Gordon on ninety-four heterosexual couples and their 5-month-old first-borns has shown that mums tend to perceive their family as a set of these couples; she will focus separately on the relationship she has with her partner and with her baby, and the relationship she observes between her partner and her baby. In contrast, dads view the family at these three distinct levels: individual, couples, family – and, as a consequence, they and their other relationships are more vulnerable to the impact of disharmony within the marital couple. This is known as the spillover effect and describes the fact that the impact of marital conflict can spill over to the rest of the family. Mums are more immune to this because they can compartmentalize their family relationships, so an argument with their partner does not impact upon their relationship with their child. But because dads see the family in its totality, rather than as a group of couples, if they fall out with their partner, the negative effects of this seep into their relationship with their child.

UCLA-based psychologist Mark Cummings has labelled this the fathering vulnerability hypothesis, due to the comparative vulnerability of dads to marital disharmony. He argues that the impact of this vulnerability on the relationship between dad and child is further exacerbated by the tendency of dads who experience emotional difficulty to withdraw from relationships. We know from Chapter Four that, unlike mothers, dads with poor mental health use withdrawal from the family as a mechanism for handling their feelings. This is also the case when experiencing marital discord but, because of their whole-family perspective, withdrawal from mum also includes withdrawal from child. The result of dad's vulnerability to this discord is that his behaviour towards the child becomes harsher and more punitive, the emotional warmth within the relationship is reduced and, ultimately, withdrawal from the family appears to be the only answer. And the outcome of this withdrawal is the risk of an insecure attachment developing between father and child and the flood of negative consequences for child, family and society that this can unleash.

This damage at the psychological level is mirrored by corresponding damage at the neural level. In their 2007 study of sixty-three children – thirty-two pre-schoolers and thirty-one teenagers – Patricia Pendry and Emma Adam of Northwestern University in the US analysed the link between the quality of the parental relationship, measured by the degree of satisfaction and frequency of conflict, and the cortisol levels of the children. Cortisol is a hormone released in the brain by the adrenal gland in response to stress. In the short term, it is highly advantageous. Its production leads to the increased metabolism of glucose to give energy, heighten memory and lower sensitivity to pain – all vital if you are to overcome the intimidating, stressful or downright dangerous situation in which you find yourself. However, in the long term, continued exposure to stress is detrimental, particularly when an individual is young and their brain is still developing, as flooding the brain with cortisol disrupts the creation of the normal neural pathways. This invariably leads to behavioural and emotional issues in child- and adulthood. In their study, Pendry and Adam found that as the level of conflict increased between the parents, so the children's cortisol levels increased, and that this effect was particularly significant in the pre-school group of children. This link to age is of particular concern as early childhood is a time when neural connections are being rapidly made – new skills are acquired and new experiences embraced – and, as a consequence, the negative impact of cortisol is at its most powerful. The disruption to normal brain development at this age has lifelong consequences. Further, the link between conflict and stress in their study was independent, meaning that the negative impact of conflict was not being buffered by any other factor. Neither the level of parental warmth and affection nor a lack of mental ill health among the parents appeared to be a protective factor. The impact of marital conflict on the children was real and direct and protection within the family was hard to find.

> [Our relationship] has changed in the way you would expect, as it is no longer just the two of us. There is someone else who we put first before either of us, I suppose. In practical terms, it means we have less time for each other. We don't really have any time on our own any more. I think we both feel it is worth it. I think we walked into it with open eyes. We do have a nice moment once in a while when we're driving somewhere and Florence falls asleep, and for a moment you can just imagine that it is just the two of us for a change, but those are few and far between.
>
> *Richard, dad to Florence (six months)*

Ultimately, the state of the parents' relationship matters because this is *the* relationship that creates the environment into which the child is born and develops, where he is nurtured and taught. The impact of the quality of the parental relationship on a child's development is beyond that of either of the relationships he or she has individually with their parents or the natural temperament of the child. It is *the* model relationship from which all other relationships will grow and against which all other relationships will be measured. It will form the bedrock of his life, will profoundly influence his mental and physical health and will greatly impact upon the success or failure of all his future relationships. In a way, the romantic relationship between parents is the practice ground for the relationship a parent will build with their child. While the relationship you have with your romantic partner is not your first attachment relationship – that would be with whoever raised you as a child – it is the first in which you have played an adult role, and while it is categorically different than that with a child, its components are the same – commitment, intimacy and passion. How well you have managed to build and maintain these three aspects in your marital life gives a good indication as to how well you will build and maintain your relationship with your child. So, if you are raising your child within a couple then the message is get your relationship with your partner right and you are already on your way to having a great relationship with your kid.

How can you achieve this? Pregnancy is about change, and if you have taken the conscious decision to have a child then you have hopefully indicated that you are comfortable with the idea of new experiences and roles. You can harness this willingness to change to instigate a discussion about how your roles and relationship may alter once you become parents. Research by sociologists from the University of Gothenburg, Sweden, has shown that the parental relationships that best navigate the choppy waters of new parenthood are those in which the parents take the time afforded by pregnancy to discuss and agree a few issues. First, what will your roles be? You and your partner will have established roles within your relationship but the addition of a third family member means that these roles need to be renegotiated. Part of this is explaining to each other what sort of parent you want to be, how you perceive the other person's role and exploring how your roles will interact productively for you and your child. Secondly, you need to acknowledge that conflicts will arise – it is amazing how important it seems to apportion blame at 3am when discussing who used the last nappy and didn't restock, to the accompaniment of a screaming baby and an unpleasant smell. By acknowledging that conflicts will occur, you can normalize this and can have an open discussion about how arguments will be resolved constructively rather than destructively – a bit of conflict management. Thirdly, you need to explore what you each expect from being a parent and what you hope your parenting style will be. One of the most difficult moments for any new parent is when their expectations are not matched by the reality – your pledge never to raise your voice can quickly fly out of the window when confronted with no sleep and an obstinate child – but it helps if you have a willing and understanding ear to help you get over this temporary obstacle. It is important that your beliefs regarding the correct way to parent align as closely as possible, so you are singing from the same hymn sheet and don't feel you are in a constant battle for parenting supremacy. Finally, if you are going to co-parent, decide to do this positively. This means supporting your partner as they parent and, if you do not agree with what you see, discussing this in a constructive and open fashion with the aim of reaching a consensus, rather than being critical or belittling. As Dan acknowledges, having children will drastically shift your focus from 'we' to 'they', so being as prepared for this as possible is key to a smooth transition for everyone.

> [Having children] is a whole other level to a marriage. It adds another deeper, more cemented layer to our marriage and to our relationship. And [you can be sure] in hell isn't about us any more!

> *Dan, dad to Daisy (six) and Bill (five)*

Apart from the fact that time will be a rare commodity after birth, focusing on your relationship before birth is effective because how you interact with your partner before birth is predictive of the functioning of your new family after birth. Families who function well act as an alliance – they are close, supportive and cooperative. All members are included in activities or discussions, everyone has a distinct role that is respected, members are able to come together with a shared goal or activity and everyone's emotions are understood and supported. The Lausanne Trilogue Play (LTP) is the catchy title of a behavioural task given to parents to allow those of us who study them to assess their joint parenting behaviour and the extent of this alliance within their family. There is a version that has been developed for use before birth, where the role of the baby is taken by a doll, and a version involving the baby for after birth. First developed by Swiss psychotherapist Elisabeth Fivaz-Depeursinge, it is of huge value because it allows us to study the family as a whole unit rather than as a set of couples, meaning that all the key players are included in the scenario, and we can try to untangle the multiple impacts they all have on each other – a much more realistic representation of the family.

Pre-birth, the parents-to-be are asked to picture the very first time they are together with their baby following his or her birth – a magical time that hopefully will get the imagination working. They are given a set of interactions to perform during their scenario to make sure the researchers can assess all the different relationships within the family – parent to child, parent to parent (the couples) and whole family. First, each parent is asked to hold the baby doll and interact with it, then they are asked to interact with the baby as a couple, and then they are told to place the baby to one side, as if sleeping, and interact with each other. Researchers are looking for how well the parents play together, how intuitively they share parenting, how warm they are towards each other and the baby and how they cooperate. It is a bit of a feat of imagination for the parents, but again and again, how they play out this scenario has been shown to be predictive of how the family will function after the birth.

In their 2013 study, Nicolas Favez, France Frascarolo, Chloé Lavanchy Scaiola and Antoinette Corboz-Warnery from the Universities of Geneva and Lausanne in Switzerland explored the value of using this test to predict how well a family would function post-birth. In their study, forty-two families carried out the test during the fifth month of pregnancy and repeated it when their child was three months and eighteen months old. What they found was that, combined with the baby's temperament, the parents' interactions before birth with the baby doll were predictive of how well the family functioned after birth. Parents who encouraged and supported their partner's interactions with the baby doll before birth continued to do so after birth, when the real baby was present. Those who worked to include everyone in the task and showed an intuitive ability to parent continued to show these abilities following the arrival of their baby.

But what was of equal interest was the unique predictive power of the father-to-be's perspective. Favez and his colleagues had asked parents-to-be to visualize their family life after the birth. To help them get a handle on this, they asked them to focus on two aspects in particular: how close it would be – that's those shared viewpoints and emotions again – and to what extent team roles would be flexible, allowing everyone a bit of precious leeway to adapt their role to suit them. What they repeatedly found was that how a father visualized his family before birth was predictive of how well it was functioning when their child was three months old. Dad's imagination is undoubtedly a powerful force, but what is it about his perspective, but not mum's, that allows it to have such a power? Favez suggested that this phenomenon was down to the difference between the way mums and dads visualize their family and the relationships within it. The father's desire and ability to envisage the family as a whole unit, rather than the series of couples more favoured by mothers, means that he finds it more comfortable to act out his parenting model at this level. His ability to conceive of his family at the whole family level enables him to have a profound influence on how well it functions. And while families are made up of their constituent relationships, the ability to picture them as a whole organism as well as individuals and couples enables fathers to have the strength to confront the difficulties that will inevitably challenge them as they move through life. In a way, dad is the family specialist.

All this prediction and preparation sounds like hard work and maybe, when there are so many other things to consider while you await the arrival of your child, a bit of overkill. But it is well worth it, because warm and supportive marital environments have an even more powerful positive impact on the relationship between dad and baby. The data backs this up. In their study of forty-four American families, American psychologists Kay Bradford and Alan Hawkins found that where emotional intimacy within a marriage was high, dads reported feeling much more competent in their role. They were more involved, felt more secure in their identity as a dad and were happier. Indeed, one role that could be particularly key is being a model of conflict resolution. Professor of developmental psychology Mark Cummings argues that the way a child reacts to its parents' behaviour will depend on the nature of their behaviour and their gender. In this case, Cummings argues that while a dad's conflict behaviour may produce a more negative reaction in his children than that of their mum, his *positive* conflict behaviours produce a similar but opposite reaction in them – their behaviours are more positive. By modelling how to disagree well – avoiding personalization, focusing on issues, looking for common ground and avoiding overt emotionality – a father both normalizes the occurrence of conflict and shows his children how to arrive at a healthy resolution. So, a father and his child stand to benefit in particular from parents taking the time to ensure their relationship is healthy and strong and conflict is effectively resolved. This means working on it while you await your child's arrival and continuing to work and monitor its health once baby is there.

Indeed, one of the few interventions aimed at trying to prevent the negative impacts of poor marital quality on families makes it clear that the power lies in prevention rather than post hoc cure. The US-based Family Foundations Intervention is a course of eight lessons, four pre- and four post-birth, which aim to help new parents deal with the strains and stresses of parenthood. Developed by Mark Feinberg and his colleagues at Pennsylvania State University's Prevention Research Center, rather than offering the traditional antenatal class fodder of nappy-change demonstrations, breathing exercises and the essential contents of your hospital bag, this programme instead focuses on giving parents-to-be tools to use when the going gets tough. So, it teaches communication skills, facilitates discussions between partners about their expectations of parenthood and encourages parents to be mutually supportive rather than undermining each other's roles. And as its developers predicted, its outcomes are not only positive but long-term. In a 2013 study of its efficacy, Feinberg and his colleagues found that of those couples who had undergone the intervention programme, parental stress reduced consistently from the point of birth, and sense of parental competency, mental health and relationship quality continually improved – positive effects that were still being felt at their child's third birthday. In contrast, the control group – who had simply received leaflets on choosing childcare – showed a consistent downward trend in all areas, despite their results on this range of measures relating to stress, mental health, relationship quality and parental competency being indistinguishable from the intervention group at the start of the programme.

And it wasn't only the parents who benefited. A warmer, more supportive parenting relationship led to positive developmental benefits for the children of these families. They were more socially competent and better able to manage their emotions – all key skills for children entering their pre-school years. The parents involved in this study were not selected because they were at high risk. The authors recognized that *all* parents find parenting tough and the skills to navigate the hurdles aren't necessarily innate – they must be taught to everyone, regardless of background. This programme worked because it was there when the couples needed it. It was there before birth to take the time afforded by pregnancy to encourage discussion and teach skills, and it was there immediately after birth to help couples utilize their learning in those first few weeks. While this is a rare intervention programme, based in the US, its findings have relevance for us all because they show the power of investing time in nurturing your relationship before your baby is born, in preparing for your new roles and developing a toolbox of skills that you can both use to ease your passage through the inevitably rocky times ahead.

All families have tough times, some very tough. Sometimes the troubles come from within – internal disagreements, difficult behaviour, health issues – and sometimes they are from outside, but families are more likely to weather these storms by remembering that the stronger a family bonds, the more likely they are to ride out the difficulties successfully. This means valuing everyone's contribution, keeping the lines of communication open, sharing your emotions and acting from a place of empathy. Think of yourself as Team Family. It is also important to have an extended network to rely upon. This does not have to be your family – there are friends and professionals who can help as well as online communities that can be an invaluable source of help, wisdom and emotional support.

Not all children arrive into the world as members of a heterosexual, biological nuclear family. But it is still the case that the majority of children live within a household that contains, at its heart, a cohabiting, parental couple. They may be gay men, adoptive or foster parents or the children may be part of a step- or extended family. For these children, the distinctions don't necessarily matter because, regardless of the fine details, these parents are the bedrock of their family and the nature of their relationship still has a profound influence on that child's development and life experience. So, while this chapter has focused on the cohabiting mum and dad experiencing the pregnancy of their biological child, the tools that they need to use, and the preparations they need to make, to ensure their relationship is a healthy one apply across the board. As parents-to-be, we rush around making our plans and enhancing our knowledge about everything from eco-friendly nappies to baby signing; very few of us stop to consider that, if we strip away all the consumer products and all the social and healthcare services, what a family is is its members and, as its founding members, parents are the model from which their family will learn and grow.

It is probably true to say that adding a baby to your relationship will mean that you have more arguments and disagreements and feel more resentful towards your partner than ever before – lack of sleep and a steep learning curve will do that to you. But it is about how you resolve these arguments and move forward that counts. And be reassured, it is overwhelmingly the case that the dads in my studies say that having a child has only deepened and strengthened the relationship they have with their partner. I'll let Noah and Adrian close this chapter with their thoughts:

> *Adrian*: We are very much in synch on parenting styles, we very much agree on what we want for [our daughter] and how to raise her. We are on a level about things because, despite being very different people, we have similar standards and outlooks.
>
> *Noah*: We have been together twenty years. We have had her for seven, so we had thirteen years before her and we had real highs and, you know, really amazing times, and that is why, when I look at her, I think, *I am really glad we stayed together*. I think it has made our relationship so much better. Because you have somebody else who takes all your attention . . .
>
> *Adrian*: . . . and brings you a huge amount of joy.

> *Adrian and Noah, dads to Judy (seven)*

PART FIVE

And Now the Fun Begins . . .

CHAPTER NINE

The School of Dad

What Dads Teach Kids

I grew up playing football, my parents coming to watch me play football and cricket ... I can't wait to experience those things with my son. I'm looking forward to teaching him things and influencing his life by being around. I want to be around him as much as I can, support him in every way I can.

Zac, dad to Aidan (six months)

Fathers love to teach. I learnt many skills and life lessons from my father that are still vital to me today. Among many other things, he taught me that you should treat others how you want to be treated, that a willingness to work hard and try your very best is more critical for success than mere intelligence and that today's seemingly overwhelming problem will seem inconsequential in a day, a month or a year. Add to

205

this the ability to lay bricks and the warning never to trust a man in brown suede shoes, and I was set for life. When I ask the fathers in my studies what they look forward to in their future relationship with their children, it is overwhelmingly the case that their vision includes the passing on of knowledge, the teaching of values, the coaching of a sport or the playing of a favourite game. Some are counting the days until their treasured toys from childhood – usually Lego, trains or Meccano – can be liberated from the loft and put to good use in a father–child celebration of play.

In this chapter, I want to look at the unique role fathers play in teaching their children. Alongside their drive to protect their children, it is universally the case that fathers play a key role in teaching and guiding their children towards adulthood and independence. But education is not just what we learn in school. Humans exist in a complex world where there are many behaviours to learn, skills to master and beliefs to interrogate and adopt. A child's future success rests not only on their intellectual and academic capabilities but on their ability to negotiate their social and physical environment, building healthy relationships with those close to them, productive alliances with those with whom they work and ensuring they cooperate to acquire the basic essentials for survival. And we know from previous chapters that fathers appear to have a unique role to play in this socialization.

Humans gain practical and intellectual knowledge by a process of social learning – put simply, they learn from other people. The world is a terribly complicated and confusing place and to learn everything we need to know to ensure survival – technological, economic, practical and social – would be impossible if we each approached gaining this knowledge by a system of trial and error. Instead, we use the fact that others have gone before us to tap into their experience, learn from them and then build on their knowledge to go forward and innovate. This may sound rather obvious and not such a big deal, but perhaps if you knew that we are the only species that actively teaches its young, you might grasp what a feat of neural and behavioural development this ability actually is. It is true to say that some animals learn by watching their parents – baby chimps can spend five years at their mother's elbow watching how she cracks a palm nut – but the parent provides no tailored guidance or feedback; the child is left to find their own way through the learning maze. There is no allowance made by the chimp parent for the different abilities that Chimp A might have from his sister, Chimp B, and identifying and nurturing his individual interests and strengths is not a priority. In contrast to your chimpanzee mother, human parents are capable of assessing their child's abilities and interests, recognizing their individual motivators, understanding the need to tailor their communication to individual learning styles and provide appropriate levels of carrot and stick to make sure skills are embedded. This all requires immense cognitive ability and, as with so much of our behaviour, our unique ability to teach is due to our large brains. Remember the couple in Chapter Eight, watching their child on the TV screen? For both of them, this task involved engaging the area of the neocortex linked to mentalizing – the ability to understand what someone else is feeling or thinking. It is this area of the brain, and this ability to 'mind-read', that also allows us to teach. Only by understanding what someone else doesn't know, what they want to know and whether they understand what we have taught them can we effectively teach them.

In many societies, the skills of a successful life are not taught in the formal setting of a classroom but out in the real world, often alongside your parents. So, Ota the Aka father ensures his children – boys and girls – learn the skills of net hunting by taking them with him deep into the Congo jungle on the daily search for food. Sigis, our Kipsigis father, ensures his sons understand the complexities of the tea trade by asking them to accompany him into the fields and to the male-only social gatherings where alliances are forged, knowledge is exchanged and deals are made. Even our apparently hands-off Bostonian lawyer, Mike, ensures that education is a priority. Beyond his financial investment in their private education, he spends his weekends introducing his children into the social world of the Bostonian business elite, ensuring they develop the networking skills that will see them in good stead in their future professional careers.

But here in the West there is an overwhelming focus on formal academic learning and achievement, often to the detriment of the attainment of other key life skills. And there is an ongoing debate about the extent to which a father has an *independent* influence on his child's academic achievements. The evidence for a parental influence is overwhelming – parents who are actively involved in their child's education at home and in school contribute positively to a child's academic success. This means providing the space and structure at home to study, taking time to read with your child, supporting their completion of homework and taking them on educational outings. But whether dad has an independent and separate role from mum has been an issue of some controversy for years. Because mums generally spend the majority of time with children, the assumption has been that this 'parenting effect' is, in fact, a 'mothering effect'. The evidence for an independent role for fathers is less strong. But absence of evidence is not necessarily evidence of absence, and with a growing focus on this aspect of dad's role comes the recognition that fathers have the potential to play an equal but critically different role in their child's academic success. And most, like Colin, are highly motivated to get involved:

> Reading books, I love books, and we've already got her a Beatrix Potter collection upstairs and Roald Dahl. I was read to a lot as a kid at bedtime and stuff, and I want to do that as well, I'd love to do that. That is what I am looking forward to, seeing her become something special and being there to support her in what she does.

> *Colin, dad to Freya (six months)*

My colleagues Eirini Flouri and Ann Buchanan are leading the quest for the all-important evidence to support the fact of a father's unique role in influencing their child's academic attainment. Working from the Department of Social Policy and Social Work at Oxford University, they believe that fathers who are involved with their children, and in particular already push their developmental and cognitive boundaries through play, *must* have a separate and equally significant influence on their children's school careers as the mother. In their 2004 study, they used data taken from the National Child Development Study (NCDS) to try to find firm evidence for their hunch. This invaluable UK-based dataset has followed 17,000 children who were born between 3 and 9 March 1958 for over forty years. Its long-term nature has meant that researchers like Flouri and Buchanan can understand what factors – socio-economic, environmental, physiological, educational and parental – have an impact on the trajectory of a child's development. Using the data regarding educational attainment, they found that, as with previous studies, the extent to which both parents were involved with their children at age seven had a significant impact on their child's academic achievements at the age of twenty. Involvement was defined by the frequency with which they read to or with the child, took him or her on outings, took an interest in his or her education and managed his or her behaviour. But if this parenting team were split into mum and dad, dad was found to have a separate and highly significant impact on the extent of his child's academic success by late adolescence. Further, this impact did not depend on the level of mum's involvement – low or high, his influence could still be felt. And despite some suggesting that fathers may have more to teach sons than daughters, his influence was the same regardless of the gender of his children.

All important and significant stuff. But what Flouri and Buchanan's study didn't manage to clear up was what this particular aspect of the dad's involvement with his child's education was. What was he doing that was different but so effective? It was left to Californian educationalist William

Jeynes to explore this question. Looking at data from thousands of people across the globe, Jeynes focused his analysis on four key potential areas of influence: fostering academic achievement, fostering psychological well-being, encouraging positive behavioural outcomes and fostering other healthy outcomes, such as being motivated to play with their kids.

What Jeynes found was wonderful and, for those of us who study dads, made total sense, because it reflected what we now know a key dad role to be: supporting his child's entry into the wider world by encouraging the development of appropriate behaviours. First, Jeynes confirmed Flouri and Buchanan's finding that dad had a significant influence on his kids' educational attainment that was separate to mum's. So that is now a given. But it was *what* dad contributed that was particularly great. Yes, he had some influence on his child's actual academic attainment, but his real power sat with the influence he had on his child's *attitude* to learning. Jeynes found that fathers had a profound impact on their children's behaviour and their psychological outcomes. Dads who were involved with their children – who fostered good behaviour, strong psychological health and a healthy attitude to life and school – taught their kids to have a good learning attitude, allowing them to reap all the benefits they could from their schooling. Jeynes argued that while the job to foster academic success was shared between mum and dad, only dad was the one who had a focus on moulding and modelling the correct learning mindsets and behaviours. He provided the foundations, the scaffolding on which a child could build their academic journey.

The role of a father in his child's academic life appears to reach its most critical point with early adolescence. At this time of whirling hormones, changing bodies and new challenges, it is often the case that a child's perception of their abilities and strengths takes a knock. But a recent study of 11,297 young American adolescents has shown that with the right sort of father involvement, a child's ability to achieve can survive this time of personal turmoil intact. It is all down to the father's power to influence his child's self-esteem, and this power lies in the relationship he builds with his developing child. American developmental scientist Mellissa Gordon, who headed the study, found that where fathers worked to build quality relationships with their adolescent child – one that was supportive, warm and lacking in criticism – not only did dad's school involvement increase but their child's sense of self was more robust and, as a consequence, they were able to achieve their full potential. It was about working to maintain that secure bond that is the foundation of all the interactions between father and child.

In contrast, Lucia Ciciolla led a team of American scientists to explore the influence that a parent's emphasis on the overwhelming importance of academic excellence had on their academic attainment. Using data from 506 early adolescents from across three American schools, she explored to what extent an emphasis on academic achievement, rather than social ability, and a high level of criticism relating to academic performance influenced a child's ability to achieve at school. What she found is a salutary lesson for all parents who, in an increasingly competitive world, may believe that academic achievement at any cost is the most important survival lesson to teach your child. Ciciolla found that where a parent placed little emphasis on educational attainment at all costs and taught that kindness and sociability were equally, if not more, important, children reported less perceived criticism, had higher self-esteem and, in fact, achieved better grades and were perceived to be academically stronger than those children who believed that their parents placed a disproportionate emphasis on achieving high grades. Now these results stood whether the parent was mum or dad. But the key issue for fathers is that where children reported that their parents did place undue pressure on them to achieve, fathers generally exhibited this behaviour at a higher rate than mothers.

So, the message for dads is this: if you want your child to achieve all they can at school, you do need to try to ensure your relationship with them is the warmest and most supportive it can be. So, take the time you have to nurture their self-esteem, involve yourself in their daily school life, teach them the value of having the right learning mindset and emphasize that academic achievement alone is of little use if you do not have the equivalent social skills – kindness, emotional intelligence and the ability to cooperate – to sit alongside those exceptional grades. Although his son Christopher is only six months old, Will seems to be on the right track:

> I think there is something about being a role model. We have talked about what type of person he might be and all the rest of it, and we want him to be his own person, but there are certain things in terms of how he treats other people, how he respects himself and, for me, that is about being the best person that I can be. So, I'm thinking about a

lot of the things I do or that I let slide. I'm changing the way I do a lot of things and trying to step up my game, because I know you can do a lot of the big one-off gestures – the big 'oh, let's take you out and have a really fun day' – but the thing that is going to make the difference in terms of how he lives his life and who he becomes is actually how I am living my life, day to day.

We all know education is about more than learning, about more than mastering your ABC or the intricacies of long division. And teaching is about more than going to school. We have already encountered in previous chapters the idea that one of the key roles for a father is to fit their children for the big wide world. To encourage them towards independence and self-reliance so they can make a success of their life. Jeynes's finding that fathers 'scaffold' their children's school experience is yet another example of this phenomenon. Dads deliver the strong foundations that enable you to get the most out of your life and build a successful future. But fathers also have much to impart outside the classroom, and for many this means an important role in teaching moral and religious values and life skills. And many dads find that to achieve this they must become, like Will, their child's role model.

I want to introduce you to a fragment of poetry:

The mother looked up in the father's face,
And a thoughtful look was there,
Jack's words had gone like a lightening flash
To the hearts of the loving pair –
'If Jack treads in my steps, then day by day

How carefully I must choose my way!
For the child will do as the father does,
And the track I leave behind,
If it be firm, and clear, and straight,
The feet of my son will find.
He will walk in his father's steps and say,
"I am right, for this was my father's way."
Of fathers leading in life's hard road,
Be sure of the steps you take,
That the sons you have when grey-haired men
Will tread in them still for your sake.

Jack is a 6-year-old boy and this excerpt is from a poem called 'Following Father'. Researchers don't know who wrote it, but we do know it was published in an English temperance journal in the late 1800s, towards the end of Queen Victoria's reign, when fathers were significantly more hands-off than today. But despite not joining in the bathing and dressing, feeding and soothing, this poem makes it clear that Victorian society's vision of the ideal father still had at its core the idea that fathers should shape their children into morally upstanding members of the world. To convey a set of fundamental life lessons that were crucial in a world where even piano legs were a bit too risqué to be on general view. The quotes from fathers that have filled this chapter show this wish still motivates dads today. If you are a father, then regardless of where you live it is likely that you, like John, who shares his aspirations below, want to influence who your children become by communicating values, broadening their life experience and being their role model for life.

I think what is important is creating an environment in which [my son] feels secure to make good decisions and think things through properly. But it is difficult. How do you help shape an individual so they are prepared to live on their own? So that they know that there is safety if they make wrong choices, that it's not the end of the world, but that they have to go through the process of coming to their own decisions? My job is guiding, influencing ... being someone that he will turn to for advice.

John, dad to Joseph (six months)

But within some modern societies, the need for a father to set an example and transmit these values is fundamental not only to their child's success but also, possibly, their survival. All fathers are involved in the socialization of their children; passing on their values and perspectives with respect to the world in the hope that their child will be better fitted to succeed in it. They achieve this through talking, teaching and modelling good behaviours and beliefs. But for some groups of fathers, the desire to do this is grounded in the knowledge that their child will inevitably experience a particular life hurdle, which, if not traversed correctly, could send them on a downward trajectory, even threaten their survival.

In their 2016 paper, 'Don't Wait for It to Rain to Buy an Umbrella', a team of American social workers, psychiatrists and behavioural scientists, led by Otima Doyle, reported on the conversations they had had with Afro-American fathers of pre-adolescent sons. They interviewed thirty fathers and asked them to respond to the question 'What values do you aim to instil in your son?' Their responses, covering themes such as culture, education, responsibility and respect, were overwhelmingly informed by their understanding that the world's response to their sons would be impacted by their race. From their own life experience, they understood that their sons would be subjected to racism and harassment, and they felt it was their duty to school them in the correct and most constructive response to these incidents. They emphasized that there was a need to furnish their sons with a set of tools to manage racism and to make them understand that they would have to work harder and achieve more than the white guy next to them to prove the racial stereotype wrong. In the words of one father, '... the path is hard ... And we'll have to also let him know that he's gonna have to work harder than the other person beside him. And their expectation is that you do not know how to talk. We do not know how to act and behave. And just make sure he knows, you can have your fun, you can talk slang ... but there is a time and place for it.' But alongside these doses of harsh reality, there was a real desire to encourage sons to have pride in their heritage and to use it as a motivation to be better. Reggie described telling his son about the history of black struggle within the US: '... they died and fought for both you and I. And so it would desecrate them if you fall short of anything other than being a man and who you are, particularly, a black man ... not only [do] you owe yourself, but you owe them as well. So, stand up and be a man.'

For these Afro-American fathers, their job was not only to bring up a son who was fully able to succeed in the outside world but to nurture and support a man who could fight the long-held stereotypes and be a proper and true figurehead for their entire ethnic group. Ultimately, as with all dads, these fathers wanted to produce an adult child who was a hard worker, had strong self-worth, respect for others and could be proud of what they achieved in life. Despite many of them not completing school, they instilled in their children the benefits of education, the need to be exposed to many different experiences and the power of formal education as a key to freedom. They wanted them, through both formal and informal education, to escape the bounds of their neighbourhood and become responsible and independent members of society. They just knew that to do this they, as fathers, had an added responsibility to furnish their sons with a set of values and life skills that equipped them to navigate an, at times, difficult and unfair world.

The majority of academic work on dads and education focuses on the biological father. But as we know from previous chapters, a father is not necessarily defined by his genetic relatedness to the child he nurtures. Indeed, due to cultural practices or life circumstance, a significant number of children grow up without the involvement of their biological father in their life. Who then provides the necessary scaffolding to support these children on their educational journey towards adulthood?

In 1998, Rebekah Coley was a graduate student from the University of Chicago. She wanted to explore how important biological and social fathers were in the education of the children of single-mother households. She could have gone down the usual route of asking mum or sitting in a corner and observing the family's daily life, but instead she did something very simple. She asked the child. She gathered together 111 8–10-year-old children, both boys and girls, and asked them to list all the people in their life to whom they were especially close. She then asked them a series of twenty-one questions about their interactions with these people, such as who teaches you, who disciplines you and who takes you out to have fun. Children were allowed to pick as many people as they wanted in answer to each question. Finally, she assessed the children's behaviour in school and gathered data about their academic attainment.

What Rebekah found was that, beyond the biological father, none of the children listed more than one other man with whom they had a close relationship, and in the majority of cases, this was their mum's boyfriend. But these men had a significant impact on the child's life. While it was the non-resident biological father who had more impact on his child's *academic* achievements – and remember, mum has the same impact as dad here – where a social father was actively involved in the regulation of a child's behaviour, the child demonstrated much better behaviour at school. Despite not being biologically related to the child, these men took on the established fathering role of scaffolding the child's psychological and behavioural development, allowing them to get the most out of their time at school.

Coley's work, and that of others, such as Rukmalie Jayakody, who look at the impact of social fathers in Western families, is important because it acknowledges that there is life beyond the biological dad, particularly in single-mother households. This can be a hard issue for biologically orientated Western minds to grasp, where it is common for biological dad still to be labelled as the 'real' father and the social father to be seen as very much the second choice, the reserve option. But just because a child is not brought up by a biological father, this does not mean they do not have a father in their life. Indeed, while it is often accepted that the lower developmental attainments of children from single-mother families is a result of a lack of a male role model, such conclusions often overlook the role of social fathers. Jayakody knows that, particularly within the Afro-American families that make up his study population, the regular absence of the biological father is often counterbalanced by a team of social fathers whose daily presence allows them to pass on vital values and morals, provide educational books and outings and support the mother in her role. These men can be a boyfriend or partner, an uncle, grandfather or close male friend. What both Jayakody and Coley know is that the father as educator comes in many guises.

* * *

Yes, we are learning with Joseph and that is changing all the time, but then you can't really apply that same learning to the second one because you're still learning as they grow up. I guess there are the general parenting skills you pick up, but then [there is the question of] how you apply that to different ages and characters. The learning doesn't come to an end.

John, dad to Joseph (four) and Leo (two)

This chapter is entitled 'The School of Dad', but it could quite easily have been called 'The School *for* Dad'. The relationship between a father and their child is not one-way, from parent to child, but mutual, and this allows for the possibility that as a father influences his child's development, so a child influences his father's. Having children sets you on a course of learning that will last as long as your lifetime, as Dylan acknowledges:

> So, the whole parenting thing evolves day to day to day. I'm sure over the next several years there will be more, it will just be ongoing. The learning curve is not as steep as when you first have them, because it was so new and so different, and your life changed immeasurably at that point. There is still an incline, but it is less of a slope. I don't think I am ever going to be able to put my feet up and say, 'That's my parenting job done.'

> *Dylan, dad to Freddie (four)*

Many men see the transition to fatherhood as an opportunity to reassess their life, to up their game and reorder their priorities. But once their baby arrives, this process of change continues. The new fathers in my studies comment regularly on the lessons that being a parent has taught them; the value of patience, the power of living in the present and the acknowledgement that lack of sleep is, indeed, an effective form of torture. But these are all the indirect results of having a child. When your child tells you that your behaviour is embarrassing or that those trousers do not go with those shoes, they are directly asking you to change your behaviour or alter your opinion. And this input, welcome or not, will continue throughout your relationship and will become more significant the older your child gets, as they hone their skills of persuasion and coercion.

Leon Kuczynski, Robyn Pitman, Loan Ta-Young and Lori Harach, from the University of Guelph in Canada, carried out a role reversal and assessed the influence that a group of 8–14-year-old children had on their parents' development. They asked the thirty couples involved to reflect upon when they had taken on board requests for behavioural change from their children, what this request had been about and which skills or behaviours their children used to persuade them to change. Unsurprisingly, the lessons that children most often imparted to their parents were about fashion and music, health and safety, appropriate behaviour (largely related to not being cripplingly embarrassing in public) and values or beliefs. Parents were largely comfortable with receiving these lessons, more so as the child aged and was deemed to be more competent, and thought they were a valuable opportunity to reflect on their own behaviour and beliefs. Children used a range of techniques to get their parents to change, from thoughtful and eloquent argument to the tried and tested practice of incessant whining or nagging. And the power of your 8-year-old's large pleading eyes to instigate change should not be underestimated. As one dad of a 10-year-old in Leon's study put it, 'What particularly caught my attention was … she did put [on] this rather important face and very serious tone in her voice. It was obvious that she was speaking from a position of authority, that she had something important to tell me. Her approach, her manner, made me listen intently.' While another father was simply bowled over by his daughter's oratorical skills: '... [her] eloquence, her ability to be very descriptive and passionate about her feelings, about what she would see, what she would experience, what she would think...' In being open to their children's influence, these fathers were taking a step towards allowing their children to be that all-important independent being, the encouragement of which is central to dad's role. They were showing their children that they respected their opinions, that they acknowledged the need for give and take in any relationship, regardless of the relative status of its members, and that their children were powerful and influential people within their relationship. By doing this, they were continuing the cycle of learning that flows between father and child but also raising their child's self-esteem and firming up the foundations of their relationship for the long term.

I think of some of the bad choices I have made in my life! And how difficult that must have been for my parents at times ... How do you cope with that? How do you enable someone to make their own choices, even when that is hard for you to accept sometimes? I guess it is that tension between shaping an individual, wanting to see all of that good potential come to fruition, but also being nervous that there is only so much you can do. He is an individual who will have his own thoughts, so how can I be a helpful influence, but allow him to make his own decision? I think that must be one of the hardest things about being a parent. Caring enough but giving enough freedom [for him] to make his own choices and mistakes.

John, dad to Joseph (six months)

223

Debates about the extent to which intelligence is inherited continue to rage. But the influence of a father on their child's knowledge and skills goes way beyond any genes he may provide. Both mothers and fathers contribute to the success or otherwise of their child's formal education, but in this, as in so much else, their roles are complementary. Fathers have a specific role in modelling the behaviour, passing on the knowledge, boosting the self-belief and creating the environment in which the child can learn. And beyond the classroom, dads are there to provide the skills, beliefs and mindsets that are vital in empowering their children to ride the peaks and troughs of their life's experience and remain mentally strong, hard-working and valuable members of society. And dads are not immune to receiving a lesson in personal grooming in return.

CHAPTER TEN

To Toddlerdom and Beyond

Dad's Role in Child Development

For the vast, vast majority of human history, fathers were believed to have no influence on their child's development. Their children's verbal dexterity, athletic prowess, aptitude for music or creative flair were all believed to be solely the result of the strong and exclusive bond between mother and child; her influence alone was key. Obviously, biological dad contributed some genes, but the environment of development was seen to be the most important factor and this was the preserve of the mother as the source of continual care and nurture.

As an evolutionary anthropologist, I find this scenario more than a little hard to swallow. It denies one of the basic rules of evolution: efficiency. Evolution is obsessed with efficiency; it is the grey-suited accountant of the natural world. It will try to reach its desired end point – always survival of the species – via the most efficient and cost-effective route available. But apparently humans were driven to solve their survival crisis by an incredibly complicated route; by creating the comparatively rare role of the hands-on dad. This meant fundamental changes in human cooperation, anatomy, mating behaviour and life history. Having largely managed to avoid each other, men and women suddenly had to cooperate on something other than sex, male brains had to evolve to teach and nurture, adults had to come to terms with a life course dominated by serial monogamy and the adolescent was born. And aren't we all pleased about that? This was a massive upheaval and quite a risk. For our species to undergo such a significant change in biology and behaviour, and for evolution to drive these changes, the human father must have had something unique and life-critical to bestow upon his children. He *must* have a role in their development. In this chapter, I want to explore what that role is, both in the early stages of a child's life and later, when he or she hits the bumpy road to adolescence. But before we get to that, we need to understand a little about the unique way humans organize their lives and why it is only human parents who have to deal with tantruming toddlers and monosyllabic teenagers.

Energy is the currency of life and 'life history' is the term given to the way an individual invests this energy during their life course. All animals have a finite amount of energy to invest and they can do this within three loose areas: growth, maintenance and reproduction. How they choose to share their energy between these three categories will have a profound influence on their life course, including when they are weaned, when they first mate, how many offspring they have at a time, how big they will grow and how long they will live.

For example, let's take two animals at the opposite ends of the size spectrum: the silverback gorilla and the field mouse. We know that, as head of his harem of female gorillas, our silverback has to grow and maintain a massive body to control his group, fight off competing adult males and protect his females and offspring. This takes the majority of his available energy. But because he doesn't invest in his children, beyond a bit of absent-minded play and the odd tolerated theft of his food, the amount he invests in actual reproduction is thankfully tiny; a few sperm. So, the majority of his lifetime's stock of energy is invested in growth and maintenance, while only a tiny proportion is reserved for reproduction. In contrast, at the other end of the scale is the female field mouse. This tiny creature is capable of reproducing a mere ten days following her birth and her lifespan is one year at most. She invests very little in growth and maintenance, but her incredibly early age of sexual maturity and her ability to produce as many as fourteen offspring every thirty-five days means that she invests a massive proportion of her energy in reproduction. Unlike the gorilla, who can live until fifty-five in captivity, this little mouse epitomizes the adage 'live fast, die young'. In contrast, despite the wish of some, who believe they have the soul of a reckless hedonist, our species is definitely on the silverback scale; a slow meander to old age, starting with a vastly extended childhood.

One other aspect of your life history, influenced again by the unique way your species apportions its lifetime's quota of energy, is the number of developmental stages you pass through, when these occur in your lifespan and how long they last. As a general rule, the 'live fast, die young' gang tend to whip through the earlier stages to arrive at adulthood, and the opportunity to reproduce, as quickly as possible. Conversely, as we know from Chapter One, those of us with large brains need to take our time reaching maturity and spend many years in the early stages.

In terms of the actual stages, the vast majority of mammals, including our fellow primates, have three: infant, juvenile and adult. They go from milk-dependent ball of fluff, to large and annoyingly energetic juvenile, to fully fledged adult. However, as is so often the case with humans, we have stepped away from this conventional pattern. Instead, we have five life history stages: infant, child, juvenile, adolescent, adult. This makes us a member of – possibly the only member of – a unique group. It is thought that only the whales and dolphins may be eligible to join us. The thing that we species all have in common is our unusually large brains, and the fact that our offspring therefore need extra time before maturity for their brains to grow and to learn to use those brains in the best way to ensure success.

Childhood is a time of exploration – of making friendships, surmounting challenges, venturing into the outside world and hopefully discovering a love of knowledge. However, within the life history world, it is less poetically defined as the time between weaning and dietary independence. Toddlers are weaned early and then need an adult to help them feed themselves solid food, as those of us who have spent many a happy hour with a stack of apples and a food blender know. This is the childhood stage. Initially, these helper adults were female relatives, but from 500,000 years ago onwards, as we learnt in Chapter One, that adult was dad.

The other unique stage is adolescence. Today, a time of deeply felt emotions, sexual, social and creative exploration and wardrobe mistakes. And for dads, like Joseph, a time to ask profound questions about how you can most effectively support your child through this challenging period, so they emerge as an autonomous adult.

I have a good relationship with my father, so it is almost an implicit criticism, but it's the ways I wish my dad would have challenged me on some of my thinking as a teenager perhaps, and didn't, probably for good reasons. I would hope to develop and foster a relationship – as they enter teenage life and start to develop their own identities, I think there is an increased question of how you navigate these questions, challenges, opportunities in life – [and] I would hope to develop a close enough relationship with them so we can have these conversations while they are still trying to work it out.

John, dad to Joseph (four) and Leo (two)

More formally, adolescence is the period defined as the time between the cessation of skeletal growth and the onset of sexual maturity. There are numerous debates as to why this stage evolved, but most likely it is to allow our massive brain to finish developing and for vital life-critical knowledge to be gathered without the distraction of an overwhelming urge to find a mate. And studies of teenage brains show us that this is indeed a time of astonishing brain development. In particular, the prefrontal cortex – the site of rational thought – is still

229

under construction, meaning that teenagers tend to respond impulsively or emotionally to situations – driven by their amygdala – rather than taking the time to consider the most sensible course of action. Sound familiar? And when mothers were still tied to the never-ending cycle of pregnancy and breastfeeding, this is the stage when the father's role became critical, reining in the most excessive and questionable behaviours and acting as teacher and guide. Research shows that fathers are as vital to the development of their adolescents as they are to their toddlers and pre-teens; their role and behaviour subtly shift as their child ages.

But let's press pause and rewind from the adolescence stage for a moment – we will return there later in the chapter – to the very early years of a child's life. We know from previous chapters that a secure attachment between father and child is vital for healthy development, and that this attachment is particularly crucial during the first 1,000 days of the child's life, as it coincides with a time of rapid brain development. In 2015, a group of Dutch scientists, led by Rianne Kok from Leiden University, carried out a prospective study of 191 children to explore the influence that their parents' caretaking behaviour had on their brain development. A prospective study means that they followed the children's development in real time, beginning the study when their subjects were just six weeks old, rather than trying to find a link by looking backwards (a retrospective study). Their first step was to gather their gaggle of very tiny babies and carry out ultrasounds of their brains and measurements of their head circumferences to get their starting point, their baseline. They then left the families largely alone for eight years, returning only at age one to measure parental sensitivity during a play session and at ages three and four to observe a parent and child problem-solving play session. After four intervening years they then visited again, when the children were eight, and scanned their brains using an MRI scanner. This allowed them to get the fine detail of brain structure, including how much grey and white matter there was. Remember, the grey matter is the neurones and the white matter the axon fibres that link neurones together, allowing different areas of the brain to communicate with each other. The theory is that the larger the amount of grey matter and the higher the density of white matter, the more 'advanced' the brain will be, because it has more neurones and those neurones are better able to communicate with each other as they have more connections. This neural intricacy allows us to display the cognitive flexibility and complexity that defines us as a species.

What they found was that those children whose parents were more sensitive during play and joint problem-solving activities did have larger total brain volume as a result of larger volumes of white *and* grey matter. As a parallel exists between oxytocin levels in securely attached parents and children, so a parallel existed between the behavioural input that the baby received from their mum or dad and the very structure of the child's brain. The evidence for the powerful effect a parent's behaviour can have upon their child's development was there before them in black (or grey) and white. I think this is amazing. The sensitive parents in this study were actually giving their children the structural foundations for life and endowing them with the neural architecture to enable them to thrive.

Becoming a toddler is a time of fast and furious change in a child's life. Gone are the days of complete dependency on mum and dad – you are starting to branch out into the world as an independent being. Your language skills are developing but doing so frustratingly slowly, so your words don't match your needs; behaviours that were once seen as cute in a baby are seen as less so in a large toddler, so you are starting to be reined in by the adults who surround you; and starting pre-school or nursery means you have to learn and adhere to endless rules about the social niceties. No wonder you have the odd tantrum. Throughout this time, a key area of your neocortex – the outer area of the brain where your higher order brain processes sit – is rapidly developing. This area, the prefrontal cortex, is where our executive functions lie. This term refers to a set of skills that allow us to respond flexibly to situations that we encounter. So, here sits our ability to problem-solve, our ability to pay attention and our ability to inhibit our less than helpful behavioural instincts. It's the bit that goes slightly haywire when you are a teenager. Executive functions allow us to meet new challenges, solve new problems and resist temptations, and in the long run those who possess a fully functioning prefrontal cortex have better mental health, can more effectively regulate their behaviour and do better at school. If children get the most sensitive and supportive input during this time then this area of the brain, and the behaviours it supports, provides a strong foundation as the child navigates life. Many fathers, like John, give this aspect of the role much thought:

I suppose the ongoing challenge for us is: how do we equip these children to grow up with increasing independence? How do we steer, direct them with the aim of increasing their independence? Certainly, the going to school was for us a stark realization that this is [Joseph's] next step towards independence from us.

John, dad to Joseph (four) and Leo (two)

And with their focus on rough and tumble play, fathers have a unique role in supporting the development of executive function in their children. We know from Chapter Seven that play is a key component in building the attachment between father and child, particularly in Western families. But the characteristics of this play – the need to pay attention to your co-player's quick moves, the need to respond in a split second to changes in direction, the need to handle your powerful emotional reactions and the need to confront and surmount physical and mental challenges – make it equally as important in the development of executive function. And we now have solid evidence that involving the child in play during the toddler and pre-school years is particularly important for the development of this suite of skills.

In 2015, a team of researchers from the University of North Carolina and New York University came together to study the impact of parental play on the development of executive function in 620 children from low-income, rural families in Pennsylvania and North Carolina. Children were observed with their parents, mum and dad separately, at the age of seven months and again at twenty-four months. During these observations, parents were tasked with playing with their children. At seven months, this was a free play session but at twenty-four months it was focused on jigsaw puzzles that were of increasing levels of difficulty, requiring mum or dad to step in and help. Parental sensitivity was measured with a sensitive parent being characterized as one who was engaged, warm, responsive to the child's cues, showed appropriate levels of excitement and supported the child's learning through play. An insensitive parent was one who appeared to be disengaged, was unaware or responded inappropriately to the child's needs, made no attempt to teach the child and remained impassive.

One year after the last play session, the researchers returned to the children and carried out tests to assess the executive function of the now 3-year-olds. The tests, made child-friendly with flip books, pictures, shapes and colours, assessed abilities in memory, attention and inhibitory control – the full triumvirate of executive function skills. The results showed that dads' influence on executive function was most evident at the 24-month play session. Children whose dads supported their play and scaffolded their learning during the puzzle task had better working memory – which is fundamental to problem-solving – attention and inhibitory control. All skills that are essential to the ability to succeed at school and navigate the social world. However, at the age of seven months, dads did not have a separate influence on executive function beyond that of mum – both parents had an equal role to play. It would appear that it is only once the child begins to explore their world and develop a life away from their parents – that is, as they become that uniquely human thing, a toddler – that dad's unique contribution to development kicks in. And again, his area of key focus is supporting his child as he or she develops the abilities – in this case the cognitive abilities – that will enable them to succeed in the world outside the front door – even if the first step is only into pre-school.

> *Dan*: I feel I am more in this for the long run. I think as they get older they will be a bit more into me. I am biding my time. I am a lot about the giving of advice. I say to them, 'I am giving this advice to you now, it won't mean much to you, but some day you will be like, "Ahh!"' So, I do feel like [I should] stick with it, not that they are going anywhere, not that I am going anywhere, but I do feel like I will get more out of it when they are slightly older.
>
> *Simon*: And I love the now. I keep thinking, *You're not going to be cuddly for ever, there is going to be a time when they are like, 'I don't really want two dads. I don't want to be cuddling you, and stop kissing me all over the face with your horrible beard.'*
>
> Dan and Simon, dads to Daisy (six) and Bill (five)

In fact, this unique and powerful contribution from fathers to their child's development extends far beyond the development of executive function. In their UK-based study, a team from Oxford University led by L. E. Malmberg explored the impact of sensitive parenting on general cognitive abilities and language development in ninety-seven families. They were interested in exploring two key questions. Firstly, they wanted to understand whether the sensitive parenting of one parent could buffer the negative impact on development of the less than sensitive parenting of the other parent. Secondly, they wanted to understand whether the links between sensitive parenting and brain development were universal, regardless of your background, or were influenced by a range of socio-economic factors, such as parents' education, socio-economic class and family income.

What they found was that the extent to which parents displayed sensitivity towards their children when they were eleven months old had an impact on mental skills at eighteen months and language development at thirty-six months, *but* this was only the case for mothers if you *removed* their socio-economic status from the mix – that is, if you pretended they all had the same background. If you put this in – that is, make your study a more realistic representation of the diversity of the human population – then maternal sensitivity had no impact on these aspects of child development. In contrast, the influence of fathers was significant *regardless* of their socio-economic status. Be they from an affluent city suburb or a deprived rural area, fathers who involved themselves sensitively in their children's lives had a profound impact on their mental development and language skills. Indeed, in the case of this latter aspect of development – the acquisition of language skills – the influence of fathers was significantly stronger than the influence of mothers. And because of their separate influence, dads were able to compensate for the impact of an insensitive mother on her child's development, meaning that dad's parenting skills were capable of buffering his child from the potential negative impact on mental development of having a less than healthy relationship with mum.

It is clear that, as a dad, the power you hold to influence your children's structural and functional brain development has the potential to provide them with the strong neural foundations that enable them to learn from their experiences and produce suitable behavioural reactions. And one of the key areas in which it can be critical for your children to get these reactions right is in social situations. We know from Chapter Five that all our fathers – Ota, Mike, Sigis and James – were focused on enabling their children to learn about and experience their social environment so that they could develop the appropriate skills to be successful adults. In this chapter, I now want us to understand what it is about the dad's behaviour and input that enable him to do this.

Adrian: She is very used to being very sociable and stuff, as well, and socially kind of forward. She is gregarious.
Noah: And also she is really likeable.
Adrian: You say that, but you are the parent.
Noah: No, but if she weren't likeable ... without a doubt, you know if people don't like your kid. But that really helps because she is fun to spend time with. I enjoy her company.

Noah and Adrian, dad to Judy (seven)

The offspring of all social animals, like Judy above, have to navigate entry to their social group and take on board the rules that govern behaviour within that group. In lower order animals, such as ants or bees, they do this by using visual and olfactory – smell-based – cues to orientate themselves. In mammals, offspring gain their first social lessons while they are still with their parents; they learn to build a mutually beneficial relationship with their mum or dad. In humans, the knowledge that we need to acquire to cement our social bonds is at two levels. The first is the more basic mammalian level where our hugs, strokes and kisses release oxytocin, which provides the neurochemical glue for our bond. And then the second is a higher level, where we employ our large neocortex – that's the folded surface of the brain where our higher intellectual and cognitive abilities sit – to develop social relationships through language and complex thought. In romantic relationships, that's the doe-eyed daydreaming, sudden urge to write poetry and an inability to stop pondering your love's myriad good points. And we need to start employing these two levels of behaviour – the hugging and the talking – at a remarkably early age. Once we hit toddlerhood, we begin to move in circles that are not necessarily populated purely by our relatives. Starting pre-school means entering a world where our potential relationships are not underpinned by genetic relatedness, and the benign acceptance this implies, so to make sure we are accepted into this group we need to employ two key skills: the ability to regulate our emotions so as not to scare anyone off and the ability to understand and abide by the rules of the setting – that is, to adopt the social norms.

Ruth Feldman's theory of bio-behavioural synchrony, which, she argues, is the mechanism that underpins all attachment relationships, implies that there is a relationship between the behavioural, physiological and hormonal measures of two tightly bonded people. But in a groundbreaking study, Ruth's team has gone on to show that this mirroring extends to the very structure of the parent's brain. They found that there was a positive link between the density of neural connections – that's the white matter – in a parent's brain and their child's ability to appropriately regulate their emotions and embrace the rules of their social environment.

As we know, in humans there are three main networks within the brain implicated in parenting behaviour: the limbic system, the empathy system and the mentalizing system – that's the basic emotions, emotional intelligence and mind-reading. The first is ancient and present in all mammals, whereas the second and third sit in the neocortex. These two systems – the basic and the advanced – are linked by two-way channels of communication, allowing the human parent to provide a multilayered parenting service. In their study, Eyal Abraham, Talma Hendler, Orna Zagoory-Sharon and Ruth Feldman focused on the density of neural connections within and between these three areas in twenty-five heterosexual biological mums and twenty homosexual biological dads, all primary carers. The Israeli team found that, regardless of whether the primary carer was a mum or dad, both the parents' behaviours and their neural structures could predict how well their child navigated the social environment of pre-school. So, the most basic of parenting behaviours – touch, simple soothing speech and gaze – underpinned a child's ability to regulate straightforward emotions such as joy. Further, the extent to which parent and child were in bio-behavioural synchrony during infancy – that's behaviours, physiological measures and bonding hormones all in synchrony – predicted how well a child could handle their more complex emotions, such as frustration and anger, and parents who were warm and positive but used suitable levels of control and employed boundary-setting – those are the social rules being enforced – had children who were well socialized within the pre-school setting.

But beyond these clear behavioural links, there was also a striking relationship between these skills and parents' brain structures. Again, those children whose parents had higher densities of grey and white matter in the emotional areas of their brain were generally more positive, could regulate their simpler emotions by self-soothing and were more socially engaged. Parents who had higher densities of grey and white matter in the empathetic areas produced children who, again, were more positive, but this time employed quite complex behaviours to regulate their stronger and more negative emotions. Finally, where parents showed good levels of grey and white matter in the mentalizing area of the brain, their children exhibited more socialization – they understood and complied with adults' requests more regularly, were willing to share, and helped and comforted others. Further, and more strikingly, there was a direct link between the density of connections *linking* the limbic and empathetic areas of the parent's brain and their child's oxytocin level at pre-school age. It's as if their parents' brains were the actual physical foundation of the child's emotional and behavioural development.

Why do these results matter? They matter because they show us how social competencies are able to cross generations. The parents in this study had advanced abilities in the emotional, empathetic and mentalizing skills that are required to be a successful, social human. And via their parenting behaviour, mums and dads were are able to pass these abilities on to their children. Secondly, they matter because the ability to grasp these basic behaviours at a young age sets you up for life. Individuals who have good emotion regulation and socialization as young children go on to achieve more in their personal relationships, education and employment as adults.

So, as a dad, it is important to nurture these key socialization skills in your children and the most effective time to achieve this is during those first 1,000 days, up to your child's second birthday. It is important that you mirror the types of social skill you expect them to display, take the time to tune into their emotions and needs so you can support them appropriately, encourage bio-behavioural synchrony through play and put in place firm boundaries for when a behaviour is unacceptable so your child gets an unambiguous message about what is good behaviour and what the world can do without. At times this can be tough, particularly if your boundaries are met with the mother of all tantrums, but by modelling what is acceptable and calling out what is unacceptable, you are bestowing a valuable gift on your child: the survival-critical ability to master the social world.

While this is the ideal, for some children, their father's circumstances may make being involved at the necessary level and time difficult or impossible. For these children, having a father who struggles to be appropriately involved in their child's life, be it as a result of work, ill health or separation, can lead to significant issues with social behaviour. One consequence of a lack of suitable father involvement is social withdrawal. The opposite of emotional engagement, social withdrawal describes a reduction in or complete lack of positive behaviours and a reduction in negative behaviours – the child turns in on themselves. It can be caused by a characteristic of the child and is seen in children who have autism spectrum disorder, post-traumatic stress disorder or an attachment disorder. But it is also seen in the children of depressed parents, the argument being that the child tries to cope with the dysfunctional relationship by mimicking some of their carer's behaviours, such as sadness, lethargy and lack of animation – a much less positive illustration of the power of synchrony. As we become increasingly aware that a significant percentage of new fathers suffer with post-natal depression and that a father's transition to parenthood can last up to two years, there is clearly a risk that a child's emotional and behavioural development can be negatively impacted by their dad's mental health during the precious pre-school years.

Several recent studies provide evidence of this. In their study of 260 infants, Finnish child psychiatrist Mirjami Mäntymaa and her colleagues found an association between the risk of a child displaying social withdrawal and a father's perception of their mental health during the year preceding the experiment. My colleague in the Department of Psychiatry at Oxford University, Paul Ramchandani, has spent over a decade exploring the impact of poor mental health and psychiatric disorders in fathers on their children's develop-ment. He has found that having a father with depression during the postnatal period increases the chances of behav-ioural conduct problems and poor language development in boys when assessed at three and a half years. Fathers who experience prenatal and postnatal depression increase the risk of their child displaying the symptoms of a psychiatric disorder at the age of seven. Why does the relationship found in these two studies exist? It may all be down to that most human of attributes – how we talk and what we talk about.

In 2012, Ramchandani gathered a group of thirty-eight new fathers together. All were the parents of 3-month-old babies, boys and girls, but nineteen of them had something else in common: they were clinically depressed. He asked all the dads to spend three minutes talking to and playing with their child without the use of toys. He recorded their interactions and then analysed the contents of their 'conversation' with their child. What he found was that fathers who were depressed tended to talk mostly about their own experiences and feelings while interacting with their child, rather than focusing on the joint experience of play. Further, their vocabulary exhibited what is known as a negative bias. They were much more likely to use negative language and be openly critical of themselves and their child. A child's ability to develop a secure attachment to their carer and develop their own mentalizing skills – those skills that enable us to understand another's thoughts and emotions – is based in part on the 'meeting of minds' which occurs during the interaction between a child and their carer. In interactions that involve a depressed father, this meeting of minds does not occur, as the father is largely self-focused, meaning that the child's attachment and mental development may be impaired.

However, if you are a father who struggles with his mental health, the story need not be one of relentless negativity. The door to contributing positively to your child's development does not close with a resounding thud on their second birthday. As we know from teenagers, the brain continues to develop and alter throughout our lives and researchers have identified other periods in a child's life when receiving the correct input can make up for the less than optimal circumstances of the past. By taking the opportunity afforded to you by the ever-developing human brain, you can seize these periods of heightened sensitivity to reassert your presence and be a positive influence in your child's life. And one of the key moments to seize is that period of rapid change and upheaval that heralds the arrival of your very own teenager.

I mentioned at the start of this chapter that we are the only species, as far as we know, to have the adolescent life stage and it is believed that this evolved to give our children time to learn everything they needed to know to succeed in our world. In the environment in which we evolved, this meant accompanying dad out into the savannah to learn the skills of tool production and hunting and taking the time to hone your social skills to ensure you could plan and cooperate successfully with your fellow hunters. All critical survival skills. Today, it might equally mean teaching them to cook, use the washing machine, involving them in a team sport or encouraging them to take on a new physical or mental challenge to broaden that all-important college application. But beyond teaching, fathers have a unique role to play in the development of that most vulnerable of teenage traits, their mental health.

As Poppy has grown up, by far the best way of teaching her things is letting her do stuff, as long as it is safe. The reverse of 'do as I say, not as I do'. Sometimes you have to let them do stuff and sometimes they might fall off things, bump into stuff and get quite upset by it. Let them be kids. You need to expose them to stuff. They are tough and they will bounce back from a lot more than you think they will. Expose them to risk and challenge by the games you play with them, the books you read to them; expose them to as much stuff as possible so that later in life they can cope.

Nigel, dad to Poppy (five) and Isabelle (two)

Life is full of obstacles, full of issues, and it is best to approach them like, 'Okay, fine, let's get on with it.' Because some people just get bogged down in negativity. I want her to always be glass half full rather than half empty.

Noah, dad to Judy (seven)

Resilience describes the ability of an individual to act and adapt positively to a difficult or challenging situation. It is the characteristic that Noah and Nigel are determined to instil in their children, despite their young age. Resilient people tend to be more socially active, are more flexible and report higher levels of satisfaction with their life than non-resilient people. One of a father's key jobs, on the behavioural evidence, is to expose his child to challenging or adverse conditions so that they develop the characteristics of a resilient person and can confront and overcome the sticks and stones that life may throw at them. This does not mean exposing your child to twenty-mile route marches in a force 10 gale but allowing your child to take physical and emotional risks in the knowledge that they can return to you as their warm and secure base.

And in an interesting angle on this discussion, a team from Shaanxi Normal University in China, led by psychologist Baoshan Zhang, argues that a father's unique ability to influence his child's mental resilience is all down to his gender.

Zhang and her team argue that resilient people tend to have masculine personality traits: social dominance, goal orientation, self-confidence, psychological capability, optimism and the ability to see the funny side. Now, she and her team are not arguing that only boys or men can have these personality traits, girls and women can too. What they are saying is that in our gendered world, these traits are seen as 'male' and, as such, men tend to adopt them and are, therefore, in a position to pass them on to their children. They asked 748 secondary school students, aged eleven to sixteen, to report on two aspects of their fathers' involvement in their lives: the extent to which they perceived him as emotionally warm and the extent to which he was punitive, or handed out the discipline. They also asked the students to indicate their level of agreement with a series of statements – for example, 'men are brave' – which would be used to assess, firstly, their perception of a male stereotype and, secondly, the extent to which they identified with a male gender role.

What they found was fascinating. As we might expect, children who perceived their father as emotionally warm exhibited higher resilience, whereas those with overly punitive fathers exhibited low resilience – warm behaviour breeds good mental health, while hostility breeds the avoidance of challenge and difficulty. But it was not simply the fact that warmth led to resilience. What appeared to be happening was that the warmth and closeness between child and father allowed a reciprocal relationship to exist whereby the child, regardless of gender, took on some of the male-gendered characteristics of their father, which, it is argued, underpin resilience. Now, such a conclusion is controversial, as it suggests those who are female-gendered are not resilient. But it is an interesting explanation for why dads do seem to have a particular responsibility for their children's ability to deal with challenge and risk and come out still smiling on the other side.

And this unique and individual influence on mental health is not limited by the culture of fathering but is universal. In populations from South and Central America to China, from Europe to America, it is powerfully the case that fathers have a special role to play in their child's future mental health. In a study with a similar finding, Argentinian developmental psychologist María Cristina Richaud de Minzi found that fathers had a separate and more profound impact on their children's mental health than mothers. In her group of 860 8–12-year-olds, Richaud de Minzi found that where the child was securely attached to their father, they had a much-reduced risk of exhibiting symptoms of depression or reporting feelings of loneliness. In contrast, children who reported insecure attachments to their fathers were much more likely to report sensations of loneliness, a fear of being alone and loneliness in their relationships with both their parents and their peers.

Why do dads have such a profound impact on teenagers' mental health? It is because of the combination of two factors: the dad's focus on encouraging social competence and autonomy and the unique environment of development in which a teenager finds themselves. Being a teenager is all about beginning to move away from the parents who have formed your environment to date and entering a new world, where your key sphere of influence is your peers. To achieve this successfully, you have to be confident in your ability to operate independently and build healthy and reciprocal relationships by displaying your best pro-social behaviours – behaviours that are positive, helpful and intended to promote social acceptance and friendship, such as empathizing, sharing and appropriate emotional control. Because your ability to do this is largely down to the attachment you form with your dad, and being unable to operate in the social world can be an alienating and stressful experience, there is a direct relationship between the relationship you have with your dad and the likelihood you will suffer from depression or anxiety.

But this relationship is not just significant during your teenage years. How you relate to your father throughout your teenage years can have long-term consequences for your physical and mental health well into adulthood. We have met the stress hormone cortisol before, in Chapter Eight. Although in small quantities it is invaluable in enabling us to overcome immediate causes of stress or threat, long-term flooding of your system with it leads to an inability to cope with stressful life events and has negative consequences for your physical health; it increases the risk of cardiovascular disease, diabetes, high blood pressure and cancer. In 2017, psychologists from Arizona State University and San Francisco University studied what impact shared father–child time during adolescence had on the cortisol levels of young adults as they carried out a stressful task. The team found that where dads reported spending time with their children – sharing leisure activities or household chores such as cooking – these children, as young adults, had lower cortisol levels having carried out a stressful task than those whose fathers had engaged less. Further, these results held across ethnic groups and whether the dad was the biological father or the step-father. Previous studies have highlighted the importance adolescents place on the amount of time their dads spend with them in assessing how important they are to their father, which has knock-on effects for self-esteem and mental health, and this study implies that this psychological well-being is underpinned by a functioning neurochemical system. So, the message to dads of teenagers is: make sure you spend one-on-one time with your child. It doesn't have to be a special activity – cleaning the car or cooking the Sunday roast is perfect. But it is a crucial time that will make them feel important to you and go a long way to reinforcing your bond, which, even though they are moving away from you, remains as vital to their well-being as ever.

But what you pass on to your child is not simply your life experience or your best recipe for the Sunday roast. Your lifetime's legacy is also written in your genes. Epigenesis is the phenomenon whereby the environmental impacts on a father's development during his childhood are capable of being inherited by his children. This is quite a hard concept to grasp. Obviously, a biological father contributes 50 per cent of his child's genes, but as genetic material – by this I mean DNA – cannot be altered during a lifetime as a result of environmental conditions, it was believed that anything a father ate, drank or inhaled before conceiving his child couldn't alter his genes and, as such, this couldn't be passed on to any children. A father could live hard and fast in the comforting knowledge that, while his behaviour might have a psychological impact on his children, there would be no fundamental change to their biology. We now know this is not the case. Characteristics that a father gains *during* his life time before he has a child *are* genetically heritable and have the power to impact both positively and negatively on his child's development.

Epigenesis does not describe an alteration in the genetic code itself – that's the DNA – rather it is an alteration to the way the gene is operated. It is a bit like the DNA being the hardware and the epigenesis is the software altering the way the gene is expressed. So, the chromatin, tasked with condensing DNA so it fits within the cell nucleus, or the histone – the protein around which DNA wraps itself – undergo an alteration, rather than the genes themselves. The software is modified rather than the hardware. I must admit, this took me a bit of time to get my head around. Maybe an example will help.

In nineteenth-century northern Sweden, the population lived under a cycle of crop failures and crop abundance, which meant, during times of plenty, they would take the opportunity to indulge themselves in some serious overeating. Two generations later, it was noticed that the grandchildren of these people had a much higher risk of dying from diabetes-related causes and heart disease than the average population. It was as if they had been enjoying a very rich diet, even though they had done no such thing. Why was diabetes, usually a disease of the obese, so prevalent in this population? The answer lay decades in the past. The environment of plenty that their grandparents had periodically enjoyed was having its impact *two* generations later, on their grandchildren's health. The expression of the grandparents' genes had been altered by their dietary overindulgence and this had been inherited by their children and then passed on to their grandchildren. This is epigenesis.

There is growing evidence that obesity, the epidemic of our age in the West, may be in part caused by an epigenetic mechanism. In one of the very first studies of its type, published in 2006, Marcus Pembrey, from the Institute of Child Health at University College London, and his British and Swedish colleagues from partner institutions decided to explore the impact that having a father who smoked during his own childhood had on an individual's body mass index (their BMI), the measure widely used in the medical profession as an indication of healthy, or unhealthy, weight. Using a vast database that had been collected as part of the Avon Longitudinal Study of Parents and Children (ALSPAC), a long-term project looking at child development, they investigated whether there was a link between the age at which a dad started to smoke and his children's BMI. Of the 9,886 fathers included in the study, 5,451 had smoked at some point in their lives. Of these, the most common age to start was sixteen, but some began between eleven and fourteen and a small but significant number, 166, reported that they had begun at younger than eleven. What Pembrey found was that the earlier a dad began to smoke in his childhood or adolescence, the higher his child's BMI. Children whose dad had started before they had reached the age of eleven were at significant risk of being obese. But this was only the case for sons; daughters were unaffected. And here we arrive at another fact about genetic inheritance. Between mum's genes and dad's genes, not all is equal.

Imprinted genes are genes that are capable of being 'silenced' in either the mother or the father. This means that while both parents may pass on a gene, depending upon which sex 'silences' their version, only the gene from one parent will be active in their child, producing a behaviour, ability, anatomical feature or disorder. This allows for the possibility that the inheritance of a trait may be the result of inheritance from only dad or only mum. Unlike the example from Marcus Pembrey's work on smoking and obesity, with imprinted genes it is not the sex of the child that affects whether a gene has an impact but the sex of the parent that counts – the same gene could be silenced in mum but not in dad, meaning only inheritance of that gene from dad will have an impact on the child; inheritance from mum will have no effect. It is argued that imprinted genes are of particular importance in the development of the brain, and it may be that fathers and mothers have 'genetic responsibility' for the development of different areas. But this work is in its very early stages and at present the most solid evidence for imprinting comes, again, from research on the genetic underpinnings of obesity. Catherine Le Stunff, from the Hôpital Saint-Vincent de Paul in Paris, and her colleagues explored the inheritance of a gene linked to the production of insulin. They found that there were two versions, types I and III. Children who had inherited the type I version from their father had a significantly higher risk of developing early onset obesity than those who had inherited type III from either parent or type I from mum. The gene was an imprinted gene, silenced in the mother and only active in the father.

The roles of epigenesis and imprinted genes in child development sit at the very cutting edge of science. It is fair to say we are still very much in the exploratory phase of understanding the extent of the impact they can have on a child's development and the different roles mum and dad might play. But as our knowledge grows, we will be able to move beyond the current focus on health – always the priority in genetic studies – to understand how dad's genes might contribute uniquely to their child's anatomical, physiological and behavioural development.

Dads have a profound and very real impact on their children's development, which ranges from the genes they inherit to the hormone levels they exhibit, from the structure of their brain to the behaviours they display, and from the mental resilience they harbour to the physical health they experience. In some cases, the impact of the father is equal to the mother, but in others – such as language, executive function, prosocial behaviours and mental health – the father has a unique and separate role to play. If you are a dad, remember that by being involved, particularly during the toddler times and teenage years, you are setting your children up for the long haul. The lessons, skills, time and experiences that you confer upon your child provide the fundamental neural, psychological and behavioural foundations on which they can build a successful and healthy life. And if these foundations are strong enough, they will last a lifetime, long into adulthood, meaning that your legacy has the potential to endure long after you have gone, in the wonderful child that you have raised.

CHAPTER ELEVEN

Dad 24345.0

The Future of Fathering

So here we are in the twenty-first century. An immense amount has happened in the half a million years since human fatherhood evolved. We've seen off all our hominin cousins to be the last ones standing (we think), we have endured numerous ice ages and populated the earth, developed villages and cities, domesticated animals, discovered complex economics, created myriad cultures and languages, pushed the frontiers of scientific and technical innovation ever forward, fought wars, negotiated peace and still found time to invent and play Pokémon Go. And throughout all this, human fatherhood has responded and, critically, endured. I have entitled this chapter 'Dad 24345.0' because, to be frank, I am unsure what version of the dad model we are on today – his immense flexibility makes it hard to keep up. But what I do know, and what hopefully is evident from the past ten chapters, is that fathers still stand at the very centre of our society. One of its critical players, defending his twin pillars of protection and teaching, and investing in his children's present and future.

In this chapter, I want to explore where the dad of today is and where he is going. When I began studying fathers ten years ago, dads were just grateful that someone was giving them some attention, and thoughts about society's view of fathers or the availability of supportive government schemes were far from their minds. But as research has accumulated, as media focus has increased and as this generation of new dads has become increasingly aware of both the benefits they bring to their children's lives and the joy and fulfilment that being a father brings to theirs, dads are beginning to be much more politicized. They are aware of their wants, needs and rights, and feel sufficiently empowered by this renewed focus to be vocal about them.

All my studies culminate in an interview. After the questionnaires, blood tests and health checks, this free-ranging, minimally structured moment of the study allows dad to be truly unrestrained. He can share his thoughts, opinions and experiences. It is a conversation that is largely dad-led and can last for several hours. However, at the end of every interview, after we have discussed the practicalities of being a dad, taken time to record birth stories, noted aspirations and fears and explored sources of anxiety and joy, I ask my final question: how do you feel our society treats fathers? These interviews are almost inevitably occasions of strong emotion – love, pride, frustration, fear – but it is this question that in many cases prompts the most passionate, and at times angry, response. For these fathers have given a huge amount of thought and consideration to their role – indeed, they feel it is sufficiently important to give their time and energy to one of my studies – but their experience is that this dedication is often unrecognized, even actively belittled. In a world where the role of mum is paramount, even sanctified, the lack of focus and support available to fathers and the enduring stereotype of the inept dad leaves many of the dads I study with the overall impression that, while paying lip service to their needs, our society would very much prefer it if they would kindly get back in their box. Aadit's feelings are a common reaction:

> I think that the UK government, or society, thinks that the father isn't needed at home, that's why a system is created with only fourteen days' leave. The impression is that the dad has to be moved out of the house as soon as possible.

> *Aadit, dad to Balan (six months)*

It is true to say that we are at a point of critical change in Western society when it comes to dads. We are on the cusp of a potential revolution and, for those of us in the field of fatherhood studies, it is incredibly exciting. In one direction lies the promised land of the involved dad – equal parent, nurturer, investor, supporter – and in the other is the more familiar land of the traditional father, ready to put food on the table and instil discipline, but existing at a slight distance to his partner and children. Objectively, we know that for the child, the family and society, a return to our evolutionary roots with a model of involved fatherhood is the way to go, but what will decide which way we turn is in part down to the individual dad. If enough dads, and mums, demand change, then change will come. But dad's ultimate fate – like every aspect of his role – is also inextricably tied to our politics and economics. For, at the end of the day, a dad cannot act alone, but must take his society with him. And it is here that the path becomes a little tricky.

Ten years ago, you could count on one hand the number of journal and press articles about involved fathering, and the term very rarely passed the lips of anyone in power. But today, the increased importance placed on the role of the father is no more clearly evidenced than with a quick over-view of the number of reports published globally by think tanks, governments and charities with a focus on dads and co-parenting. In the past few years we have seen, among others, the Royal College of Midwives, MenCare, Working Families, the International Men and Gender Equality Survey, the US Congressional Research Service, the National Fatherhood Initiative and the UK government's Women and Equalities Committee all focus their resources on drawing up reports about the state of fathering globally. They have focused variously on the role for the father in childbirth, the balance between a father's work and family life, the drive towards true equality in the home and the global state of fathers' rights to paternity leave. This is all immensely encouraging as, after years of failing to register on anyone's radar, dads are now the focus of discussion. And this flood of interest is an acknowledgement, however belated, that they have something vital to contribute to their children and our society. But, while hugely welcome, the impact of these reports on actual practice makes it clear that we have some way to go before everyone is singing from the same song sheet and before the aspirations of today's dads are matched by reality. The starkest representations of this can be seen in two reports: one that is UK-focused and impacts the very start of a father's journey; and the other that considers the gap between the status of mothers and fathers globally.

In 2010, the Royal College of Midwives published their report, 'Midwifery 2020', which set out their vision for the practice of midwifery in the UK by 2020. It was a report that explicitly listed dads as a target reader group. It referred to the increasing scientific evidence for the impact of father involvement on the health of the mother and child and on his child's development. It highlighted the period around birth as a 'golden opportunity' to offer fathers advice and support and ease their journey into parenthood. It explicitly stated the need to engage with fathers as important figures in maternity care, not only to elicit their feedback on how services could be improved but to motivate them to be the drivers of change. And as a result of all these factors, it argued that midwives should be working with fathers to encourage their involvement and support. All laudable aims. But the reality at present, in 2017, three years from their deadline, is rather a long way from this vision. Unfortunately, words have not been followed by action.

> I think the thing that struck me was you are either treated as a couple having a child or as a mother. There is nothing focused on, and no support groups for, fathers. There is nothing to help you prepare for your role.

> *John, dad to Joseph (six months)*

The voices of the fathers in this book make it clear that, despite the best aims of policymakers, they are not equal players in the process of pregnancy and childbirth, and a considerable number feel actively excluded from the birth of their child. My experience is that this is not due to a lack of enthusiasm on the part of dads to step up and assume a role during this time. Nor do I believe that the blame should be laid wholesale at the door of the midwives or health practitioners. If a father requests support or to adopt a particular role during birth, the vast majority of midwives are happy to help him make it happen. No, the fault lies higher up the chain, within governments and societies whose engrained cultural beliefs mean that they are resisting both the scientific evidence and the increasingly loud calls for change. And this is no more strongly evidenced than within the UK. Bob's experience is an upsetting reminder of this:

> Kate was offered support when we had the miscarriage. We went to the hospital and they talked to her there and said to give them a call whenever she wanted, but I was offered nothing. Again, it was a mum's thing. Mums have miscarriages, dads don't.

> *Bob, dad to Toby (four) and Harry (sixteen months)*

Within the UK, the National Institute for Health and Care Excellence (NICE) consults on and develops guidelines for clinical care within the National Health Service. Their guidelines for the care of women during birth were published at the end of 2014 and run to a hefty eighty-eight pages long. The document details best practice during birth and provides healthcare staff with guidance when decisions need to be taken as to the next steps in clinical care. There is now a growing body of evidence that the healthcare outcomes for mum and baby are significantly improved if dads are included in discussions and decisions taken as labour proceeds. But nowhere in NICE's 88-page document are the terms 'dad', 'father' or 'partner' referenced. Even if we forget the fact that fathers, who are invariably in the room, might have a need, and arguably a right, to be included in discussions and decisions about the birth of their child, and we look at this issue exclusively from the point of view of mum and baby, this is a glaring omission. NICE argue that their guidelines are patient-focused and, as far as the NHS is concerned, it is the mother and baby exclusively who are the patient in the context of birth. But the *sole* aim of medicalized childbirth is to increase the chances of survival for mum and baby. When a major factor that positively impacts this chance – having an involved and informed father – is excluded, that should be of concern. It is true to say that an expectant father is not the focus of *medical* care, but he is more than a visitor, a hand-holder or a bag-carrier, and it is arguable that there should be a duty of care towards him as well, to monitor his welfare. The previous chapters have made clear that there is powerful evidence that birth is a life-changing occurrence for mum and dad alike – biologically, physiologically and psychologically – so it would seem the least we can do is make the care of both during birth of paramount importance.

If you engage the social context of the mother – her family – you are tuning in to the way human beings behave. Extracting a mother and sticking her in a health facility is less effective, but that is the worldwide global norm. That is the model that is being exported and distributed around the world [and changing] it is very complicated, it is ridiculous.

Duncan Fisher, OBE, Family Initiative

The consequence of a world run on an outdated maternity care model that is out of step both with the evidence and with the desires of parents is a world in which dads are still absent from many of our conversations about parenting. Despite the unequivocal evidence that dads want to be hands-on, that involved fathering improves a child's developmental out-comes, increases maternal and infant health, reduces violence towards women and girls and increases sexual equality in the home and workplace for the long term, the message is slow to infiltrate the corridors of power. MenCare's 2015 report 'The State of the World's Fathers' was the first of its kind to carry out a global assessment of the status of fathers – the extent to which they are included, supported and advocated for. It found that there were still considerable barriers to dads being involved. Some of these were economic, particularly in poorer countries, but the largest hurdle was in our minds. The hurdle is social and cultural; the belief that men work and women care and that they are biologically incapable of carrying out each other's roles. In many countries, women have begun to break through this particular barrier within the working world, although the glass ceiling is proving to be considerably thicker than we thought, but men are a long way behind their sisters on this particular ladder. They are yet to convince the majority that men can care.

Combine this societal block with a world that is increasingly focused on individual rather than governmental responsibility – leading to cuts in social and healthcare services and a rise in unstable employment practices – and you have a world where, despite the vast majority of men stating that they would work less if it meant they could spend more time with their kids – ranging from a low of 61 per cent in Croatia to a high of 77 per cent in Chile – any form of statutory paternity leave is only present in ninety-two of the world's 196 countries. It is still the norm rather than the exception outside the West that the majority of men take no time off work after their children are born. This disparity between what men want and their reality must be laid, to a great extent, at the feet of our society. This lack of equality, and the impact it has, is regularly reflected in the experiences of fathers:

> Things are getting better for fathers in terms of their rights, but there is still a long way to go. I couldn't afford for Clare to go back to work after six months and for me to take six months off, it's just not feasible with a mortgage and stuff. Yet this is the time you miss the most, you miss all the little things.
>
> *Dylan, dad to Freddie (six months)*

Because when you do support fathers, recognizing their importance and their need to be involved and providing the legislative and financial framework to empower them, revolution results. Even in that most individualistic of societies, the United States of America.

The US is the richest country in the world but, when it comes to parental leave, it has the dubious honour of being among a handful of countries that offers the fewest rights. Since 1993, women have been entitled to twelve weeks of unpaid leave for each newborn or newly adopted child, but stipulations relating to the nature and duration of your employment mean that not all new mums are eligible. The federal nature of the political system in the US has meant that some states have voted to override a number of these restrictions, but in only three states has any legislation been passed that requires maternity leave to be funded, and in those cases the onus is on the employer, rather than the state, to carry the cost.

But for some employers, an understanding of the strong link between commercial success and happy employees with well-balanced home and work lives has meant that they have proactively taken on this new responsibility. In April 2017, global management consultancy EY rolled out a new parental leave programme that meant that, for the first time, dads and mums were offered the same package of paid parental leave. Within the US, this meant that the generous sixteen weeks of leave on full pay that had previously only been offered to mum was now also an option for dad. This is an astonishing leap in corporate culture, not only within the US but globally. Within the first year of the programme, EY reported that on average new dads were taking six weeks of paid leave and eighty-two employees took the full sixteen weeks. And for EY, bringing equality to parenting rights and providing the financial support to make sure that it was accessible to all, regardless of income, was a no-brainer. A firm like theirs, which exists within the service industry, knows that their people are their product, so ensuring their well-being at the very start of their parenting journey means a workforce of contented, and extremely loyal, employees.

EY's model of equality between the sexes is beginning to be copied within other organizations, but it is a practice still largely restricted to the professional market, where a shortage of the best candidates means firms have to compete to provide the most attractive benefits package. This can result in extended paternity leave being the preserve of a privileged few, rather than all. And while on average EY's new dads took up more leave after the introduction of the new scheme, it was still the case that only 38 per cent took more than six weeks, regardless of the economic support. Why is this? It could be that, while dads talk the talk of the involved dad, they are reluctant to put words into action. But the evidence would suggest otherwise. For, where fathers have a period of financially supported leave, ring-fenced for their sole use, the rate of uptake of extended paternity leave is astonishing. But the dads of EY are still embedded in a culture of employee presentism, where presence rather than outcomes is the true measure of success. Yet, empower men – with a bit of stick and a lot of carrot – to fight back against this attitude, and the rush to be there for their children is overwhelming.

In January 2006, the Quebecois government legislated for a period of financially supported, ring-fenced paternity leave and the statistics speak for themselves. In the first year of the programme, Quebecois fathers had increased their uptake of paternity leave by 250 per cent. The length of that leave was increased by 150 per cent from two weeks to the full five weeks of paid leave that was available under the new scheme. Further, long after the leave had ended, dads were still partaking in household chores at a rate that was 23 per cent higher than their counterparts who had not taken the leave. Combine this with research from other studies that shows that if a son sees his father share in domestic work and childcare he is significantly more likely to do the same when he is an adult, and we have an influential mechanism for rebalancing gender inequality. These results stand in contrast to those from other Canadian provinces where dedicated paid paternity leave is not an option; here, less than one in five fathers takes any form of paid paternity leave.

Why is non-transferable paid paternity leave so effective at changing the culture of fathering? It could be that its father-exclusive label reduces the stigma of taking it within the workplace – it becomes a societal expectation, and fathers feel emboldened to ask for their right. It could be because not taking something that is exclusively yours – there is no chance of anyone else being able to take it – means that there is guilt attached to refusing to enable your child to spend time with you during his or her formative years. And it is definitely because it is economically supported. The Quebecois authorities have seen fit to fund the scheme to the extent that 70 per cent of a dad's income is paid, up to a weekly cap of $767. Fathers can rest easy in their role of carer, safe in the knowledge that the bills are being paid.

It is this willingness to throw their legislative and economic might behind the scheme that has made the Quebecois system so successful. In adopting this model, they are following in the well-trodden footsteps of the Nordic countries, such as Norway and Sweden, who have practised a system of paid 'use it or lose it' paternity leave for a considerable number of years. In Sweden, where the very first paternity leave was introduced in 1974, ninety of the 480 days of parental leave are ring-fenced for the dad, although he can take more, and on average dads will be the primary carer for 25 per cent of the parental leave period – that is 120 days. In Norway – dad-friendly since 1993 – parental leave is forty-six weeks at full pay, and up to fourteen weeks of these are reserved for dad. And I would argue that it is this sort of scheme – which provides appropriate legislative and financial support – that other countries, including my own, are going to have to mimic if we are to put our money where our mouth is and truly adopt a model of involved, and supported, fathering.

Having taken the temperature of dads-to-be, fathering organizations and employers, it is clear that the consensus among those of us who work with dads and are alive to their reality is that it is only with adequately funded, non-transferable paternity leave that fathers will be empowered to becoming more involved in the home, caring for their children and contributing to domestic life. The barriers to greater involvement are largely economic and cultural, and with these hurdles swept aside it will be easier for fathers to assert their rights to be present for their children from the very start. And maybe we also need to step back and let evolution take its course. Because all this cultural baggage is just that: baggage. Baggage is easy to shed if there is enough of a desire to do so. Compared to the power of biological evolution – the mechanism that has created us as a species and positively selected for involved fathers – culture is just the surface gloss. Biology trumps culture every time.

The power rests with fathers and their overwhelming love for their children because, after ten years of work, the evidence of academics and the lobbying of interest groups alone has made little headway in changing the culture among those who make and communicate policy. A lot of reports have been collated, meetings attended and coffee drunk, but progress has been frustratingly slow. So, it's time for a change of tack. From here on in, with our support and robust evidence, the drive and initiative is going to have to come from dads. It's time to man the barricades and get political. And luckily, there is an indication that this new generation may be more willing to voice their needs and desires when it comes to the importance of their role than any previous generation. My own experience interviewing younger fathers is that they are more switched on about what they can bring to their children's lives, what their rights as dads are, and are more assertive in voicing these to their employers and the professionals they encounter. A recent study of 1,043 City of London professionals, a group we may imagine to be driven by career ambition, found that among the new generation of men, aged between twenty-one and thirty-five, 40 per cent stated that they had very little interest in climbing the career ladder to senior management, preferring to work a job that allowed space for a better work–life balance.

I am hopeful that this current focus on the culture of fathering is not just a passing phase, but that we are in the midst of real societal change. And one of the aspects of that change that gives me cause for optimism is that the change is no longer local but global. As a consequence of social media, ideas and knowledge generated in our backyard can reach the rest of the world in a matter of seconds. And, in turn, we can see how others are pushing the boundaries and making change happen. While social media can have its downsides, what it has allowed us to do is break down the barriers of distance, language and culture to gain an insight into how our fellow humans live life. And that includes fathering. Before the advent of YouTube, we would have had little idea whether the beliefs we were developing about fathering – that it can be hands-on without threatening your masculinity – were unique to us. But today, simply try typing 'dads dancing with babies' into YouTube to join the hundreds of thousands of people around the world who have been uplifted by the sight of a group of thirty-something dads dancing in perfect time, in a school hall, babies strapped to their chests. Or if you want to share in some fathering knowledge, try viewing the many videos teaching dads how to do their daughters' hair. The fact that these videos have views in the tens of thousands are testament to the thirst for information about being a fully involved, hands-on dad.

Whether they are biological fathers, stepfathers, adoptive or foster fathers, or legal guardians, whether they are brothers, uncles or grandfathers, and whether they live with their children or not, men's and boys' participation in the daily care of others has a lasting influence on the lives of children, women and men, and an enduring impact on the world around them.

MenCare 2015, 'The State of the World's Fathers'

Fatherhood will always be changing, that's part of its job description. At the moment, we are focused on trying to create the environment in which fathers can truly be involved with their children. But who knows what curveballs will be thrown at our species in the coming years? The fact that we seem to be living through particularly unstable times means anything could happen, the magnitude of which could take our eye off the ball. But I hope not. I hope that, with the increase in our knowledge, the desire of men to step up and the power of social media to spread our message around the world, whatever life throws at us, we will continue to pursue our goal. And that goal is actually very simple: to recognize that fathers are important to us all; individually and as members of society. And to create an environment in which they can be free to fulfil their evolved role. To protect, to teach and to tickle their children until they are incapable with hysterics. That's the goal.

AFTERWORD

So, there we have it. Everything I can tell you about everything we, at the scientific end of things, know about being a
father today. What have we learnt? That since his evolution
half a million years ago, regardless of his environment, dad
has been using his immense flexibility to ensure that he
always fulfils his twin goals of protection and teaching. That
his role has been shaped by a combination of forces, both
social and biological, so that how he fathers is wonderfully
diverse. That all fathers are motivated to care and invest
by the same set of wonderful chemicals that, along with
significant brain changes, mean that becoming a parent is
just as biological and psychological an experience for dad
as it is for mum. That dad is an essential and integral part
of the parenting team needed to raise a healthy child, but
that who dad actually is is not bound by biological relatedness; it is fulfilling the role that counts. That the involved
father is not just a male mother, but that he carries out his
task in a unique way, with a particular focus on preparing
his child for the outside world. And that being a dad is a
role that never ends; he is essential both to the developing

social skills of his toddler and to the mental resilience of his teenager.

I said at the start of this book that I had three key aims. The first was to shift the focus away from the so-called deadbeat dad, who has been the subject of headlines and studies for too long, to the – thankfully much more prevalent – stick-around dad. He who reads bedtime stories, prepares packed lunches and locates that rogue school sock. I wanted to rebalance the record on dads because I believe that they are not who we currently think they are. Dads – related or not, cohabiting or not and even one or many – are special and unique. They are a physiological and psychological phenomenon, they are flexible, they are developmental boundary-pushers, they are carers and, in the vast majority of cases, they are *there*.

My second aim was, through my studies and those of my colleagues, to reassure fathers-to-be, new dads and established dads about their thoughts, feelings and experiences. To pinpoint the moments of tension or difficulty, to highlight the common feelings or thoughts, to explain the biology that is going to give them a helping hand and to reassure them that there is no right way to father, but that evolution has fitted you to be the best dad you can be for your child. And to give you permission to be silly and fun in the knowledge that you are playing a vital role in your child's development.

My last aim was to educate society. Dad is an integral part of every culture around the world but, compared to mum, generally we know so little about him. But we all have experience of either being or being with a dad, even if they are not ours, and we should really know more about them. That they have an impact on our society individually, as a parent and as a member of a family; they have something to offer us all. That they need our recognition, acknowledgement and support.

And now you have read this book, I need your help to tell the dad story. So much has changed for dads in the ten years that I have been working with them and much of this has been driven by the men themselves, asserting their needs, rights and desires to be involved. But there is still so much to do. The science is there, we just need to encourage society to catch up. So, please pass on your new-found knowledge and, if you are a dad, be proud of who you are. You are the wonderful culmination of half a million years of evolution, selected for *because* you matter. But don't take it from me. Take it from a real expert, John, dad to 4-year-old Joseph and 2-year-old Leo:

> Take confidence, you have an important role to play. Don't feel belittled … It is an amazing opportunity, an amazing responsibility. Seize it.

I couldn't have put it better myself.

Acknowledgements

My first thanks need to go to my agent, Sally Holloway of Felicity Bryan Associates, who managed to see some promise in a very dry academic manuscript, beat some popular-science writing sense into me and has been there for help and advice throughout the completion of this book. Secondly, I would like to thank my editor, Claudia Connal at Simon & Schuster, for all her gentle guidance and excellent editing. She has been incredibly good at spotting academic waffle and keeping me on track. My unending thanks go to my boss at Oxford, Professor Robin Dunbar, for being an inspirational scientist and author, supporting me throughout my academic career and allowing me to spend some time looking at dads when, really, I should have been doing something else. I also need to thank the members of my research group, the Social and Evolutionary Neuroscience Research Group within the Department of Experimental Psychology, for their helpful discussions. In particular, my thanks go to Dr Ellie Pearce, who read and commented on early chapters of this book. I need to thank the National Childbirth Trust, and, in particular, Fran Hill and Jenny Barrett, who helped me to recruit dads and gave their input on survey design for my studies. I need to thank my funding body, the British Academy, for financing my first study and setting me on the road to fatherhood research. I need to thank my friends for always asking how it was going and offering tea and cake when the going got tough. In particular, my best friend Ffiona, who 'entertained' herself on her many transatlantic flights with drafts of early chapters. To my work colleagues Moose, Bear and Sam: what they lack in conversation they make up for in slobber and hugs. And to all my family. But, in particular, to my mum and dad, who brought me up to believe that learning was a joy, who supported me emotionally and often financially through my degrees and who, by being amazing grandparents, enabled me to return to work and pursue my research. They have also been willing guinea-pig readers for many theses and book drafts – hopefully this was a bit easier to read than the PhD. To my beautiful stepdaughter, Lydia, and my gorgeous daughters, Hebe and Kitty. They are the point of my world. And to my husband, Julian. He was the inspiration for this book and has always been my greatest love and support. Thank you.

Sources of Help and Support

Fathering Organizations

The Fatherhood Institute

www.fatherhoodinstitute.org
A UK-based 'think and do tank'. They carry out research, lobby for policy change, collate research findings and work with families and organizations.

Dads4Kids Fatherhood Foundation

www.dads4kids.org.au
An Australian-based organization that provides information, courses and support for dads.

The Fathering Project

www.thefatheringproject.org
An Australian-based organization whose aim is to inspire and equip fathers and father figures to engage with their kids.

Father & Child

www.fatherandchild.org.nz
New Zealand-based organization that provides information and support with the aim of empowering men to be the most effective and engaged dads they can be.

Platform for European Fathers

www.europeanfathers.wordpress.com
An umbrella organization comprising twenty-five organizations from sixteen European countries that aims to advance the interests of fathers in the European Parliament and promote involved fatherhood.

OxPIP: The Oxford Parent Infant Project

www.oxpip.org.uk
A UK-based organization that provides therapeutic services to help parents build healthy and loving relationships with their children.

NorPIP: The Northamptonshire Parent Infant Partnership

www.norpip.org.uk
A UK-based organization that provides therapeutic services to help parents build healthy and loving relationships with their children.

Anna Freud National Centre for Children and Families

www.annafreud.org
A UK-based charity that focuses on children's mental health. They run a national Parent Infant Project that provides therapeutic interventions for parents who may be struggling for various reasons or who are finding it hard to build healthy relationships with their children.

Families Need Fathers

www.fnf.org.uk
A UK-based charity that supports all those affected by separation to maintain contact with children.

Kidz Need Dadz

www.kidzneeddadz.org.nz
A New Zealand-based organization that aims to support and educate dads about the importance of engaging with their children.

Family Included

www.familyincluded.com
A global organization that works to engage fathers in maternal and newborn health around the world.

Dad.Info

www.dad.info
Europe's self-proclaimed largest advice and support website for dads.

Father a Nation

www.fatheranation.co.za
A South African-based organization that provides community programmes aimed at equipping men to be fathers.

Dads Group Inc.

www.dadsgroup.org
An Australian-based social networking site that puts local dads in contact with each other and encourages the formation of dad support groups.

Fatherhood Global

www.fatherhood.global
A website that brings together the results of research being carried out by fatherhood researchers around the world.

Dads House

www.dadshouse.org.uk
A UK-based organization that supports single, primary caring fathers.

Dads in the Picture

www.dadsinthepicture.co.za
A South African-based organization founded by fathers that supports and empowers dads to be more involved in their families.

Fathers Network Scotland

www.fathersnetwork.org.uk
A Scottish organization that carries out research and provides information, advice and events to support fathers from all walks of life.

National Childbirth Trust

www.nct.org.uk
A UK-based campaigning and educational charity that provides advice, support and training to new parents. Focuses explicitly on the first 1,000 days.

The Lions Barber Collective

www.thelionsbarbercollective.com
An international group of barbers who are trained to listen to and support men who are experiencing poor mental health, including postnatal depression, anxiety and post-traumatic stress. Barbers who are involved in the collective display the collective's logo in their window.

Podcasts and Blogs

The Average Father

www.theaveragefather.com
A podcast produced by Canadian Tony Morrow by dads, for dads and about fatherhood.

Brand New Father

www.bnfpodcast.com
Blog and podcast by a new dad relating his experiences as he begins his fathering journey.

The Poppin' Bottles Dad Cast

www.poppinbottlesdadcast.com
Seventy-minute podcasts that give insight and advice about being a dad. Presented by two self-proclaimed Super Dads.

The Life of Dad Show

www.lifeofdad.com/podcasts/
Interviews with well-known fathers.

The Good Dad Project

www.gooddadproject.com/podcast/
Described as a movement and community of fathers, this podcast claims to break down the common challenges of being a father, making them easy to understand and making dads feel less alone.

Beardy Dads

www.beardydads.co.uk
Two UK-based dads who discuss topics that will interest fathers.

Modern Dads Podcast

Real-life stories about parenting and fatherhood from a group of New York-based fathers.

Simple Man's Survival Guide Podcast

A humorous look at life from a middle-aged dad from the Midwest of America.

Dad's Guide to Twins

www.dadsguidetotwins.com/category/podcast/
A podcast specifically for dads who are experiencing the unique demands of being a parent to multiples.

Geek Dad

www.geekdad.com
Fathering and technology. What more could you want?

Father Nation

www.fathernation.com
Interviews about the fathering experience, with advice on how to be a better dad.

The Dad Podcast

www.thedadpodcast.com
Hosted by stand-up comedian Justin Worsham. Entertaining and informative, with a regular guest spot for a family psychologist.

INDEX